WESTERN thinking about Japanese politics and government has frequently gone astray because of the habit of over-simplification and of trying to classify Japanese institutions and methods into purely European or American categories. On the one hand errors arise from assuming that Japan is still basically a feudal military nation with only a thin veneer of modern capitalism; on the other hand much confusion has come from regarding Japan as simply another totalitarian nation without noticing how markedly its organization differs from the political systems adopted in Fascist Italy or Nazi Germany.

The present study is a pioneer attempt to correct these misconceptions by analyzing the numerous measures of state control which the Japanese Government has increasingly introduced, especially since 1931, in the fields of industry, trade, finance, agriculture, social affairs, national defense and public opinion. It also indicates how in many of these measures Japan has often adopted the same methods, and from the same motives, as the United States and other democratic countries. The author, who is Assistant Professor of Oriental Affairs at Pomona and Claremont Colleges, has long specialized in the study of Japanese politics and methods of economic control. The study forms part of the Institute of Pacific Relations Inquiry described on the back flap of this wrapper.

INSTITUTE OF PACIFIC RELATIONS
INQUIRY SERIES

THE INSTITUTE OF PACIFIC RELATIONS

The Institute of Pacific Relations is an unofficial and non-political body, founded in 1925 to facilitate the scientific study of the peoples of the Pacific Area. It is composed of National Councils in eleven countries.

The Institute as such and the National Councils of which it is composed are precluded from expressing an opinion on any aspect of national or international affairs; opinions expressed in this study are, therefore, purely individual.

NATIONAL COUNCILS OF THE INSTITUTE

American Council, Institute of Pacific Relations

Australian Institute of International Affairs

Canadian Institute of International Affairs

China Institute of Pacific Relations

Comité d'Études des Problèmes du Pacifique

Japanese Council, Institute of Pacific Relations

Netherlands-Netherlands Indies Council, Institute of Pacific Relations

New Zealand Institute of International Affairs

Philippine Council, Institute of Pacific Relations

Royal Institute of International Affairs

U.S.S.R. Council, Institute of Pacific Relations

GOVERNMENT IN JAPAN

RECENT TRENDS IN ITS SCOPE AND OPERATION

GOVERNMENT IN JAPAN

RECENT TRENDS IN ITS SCOPE AND OPERATION

By
CHARLES B. FAHS
Assistant Professor of Oriental Affairs
Pomona College and Claremont Colleges

I. P. R. INQUIRY SERIES

INTERNATIONAL SECRETARIAT
INSTITUTE OF PACIFIC RELATIONS
PUBLICATIONS OFFICE, 129 EAST 52ND STREET, NEW YORK
1940

COPYRIGHT, 1940, BY THE SECRETARIAT, INSTITUTE OF PACIFIC RELATIONS
PRINTED IN THE UNITED STATES OF AMERICA
BY THE HADDON CRAFTSMEN, INC.

FOREWORD

This study forms part of the documentation of an Inquiry organized by the Institute of Pacific Relations into the problems arising from the conflict in the Far East.

It has been prepared by Dr. Charles Burton Fahs, Assistant Professor of Oriental Affairs, Pomona College and Claremont Colleges, California.

The study has been submitted in draft to a number of authorities including the following, many of whom made suggestions and criticisms which were of great value in the process of revision: Dr. Harold S. Quigley, Dr. Kenneth Colegrove and Mr. Cabot Coville.

Though many of the comments received have been incorporated in the final text, the above authorities do not of course accept responsibility for the study. The statements of fact or of opinion appearing herein do not represent the views of the Institute of Pacific Relations or of the Pacific Council or of any of the National Councils. Such statements are made on the sole responsibility of the author. The Japanese Council has not found it possible to participate in the Inquiry, and assumes, therefore, no responsibility either for its results or for its organization.

During 1938 the Inquiry was carried on under the general direction of Dr. J. W. Dafoe as Chairman of the Pacific Council and in 1939 under his successor, Dr. Philip C. Jessup. Every member of the International Secretariat has contributed to the research and editorial work in connection with the Inquiry, but special mention should be made of Mr. W. L. Holland, Miss Kate Mitchell and Miss Hilda Austern, who have carried the major share of this responsibility.

In the general conduct of this Inquiry into the problems arising from the conflict in the Far East the Institute has benefited by the counsel of the following Advisers:

Professor H. F. Angus of the University of British Columbia
Dr. J. B. Condliffe of the University of California
M. Etienne Dennery of the Ecole des Sciences Politiques.

These Advisers have co-operated with the Chairman and the Secretary-General in an effort to insure that the publications issued in connection with the Inquiry conform to a proper standard of sound and impartial scholarship. Each manuscript has been submitted to at least two of the Advisers and although they do not necessarily subscribe to the statements or views in this or any of the studies, they consider this study to be a useful contribution to the subject of the Inquiry.

The purpose of this Inquiry is to relate unofficial scholarship to the problems arising from the present situation in the Far East. Its purpose is to provide members of the Institute in all countries and the members of I.P.R. Conferences with an impartial and constructive analysis of the situation in the Far East with a view to indicating the major issues which must be considered in any future adjustment of international relations in that area. To this end, the analysis will include an account of the economic and political conditions which produced the situation existing in July 1937, with respect to China, to Japan and to the other foreign Powers concerned;

an evaluation of developments during the war period which appear to indicate important trends in the policies and programs of all the Powers in relation to the Far Eastern situation; and finally, an estimate of the principal political, economic and social conditions which may be expected in a post-war period, the possible forms of adjustment which might be applied under these conditions, and the effects of such adjustments upon the countries concerned.

The Inquiry does not propose to "document" a specific plan for dealing with the Far Eastern situation. Its aim is to focus available information on the present crisis in forms which will be useful to those who lack either the time or the expert knowledge to study the vast amount of material now appearing or already published in a number of languages. Attention may also be drawn to a series of studies on topics bearing on the Far Eastern situation which is being prepared by the Japanese Council. That series is being undertaken entirely independently of this Inquiry, and for its organization and publication the Japanese Council alone is responsible.

The present study, "Government in Japan—Recent Trends in its Scope and Operation," falls within the framework of the second of the four general groups of studies which it is proposed to make as follows:

I. The political and economic conditions which have contributed to the present course of the policies of Western Powers in the Far East; their territorial and economic interests; the effects on their Far Eastern policies of internal economic and political developments and of developments in their foreign policies vis-à-vis other parts of the world; the probable effects of the present conflict on their positions in the Far East; their changing attitudes and policies with respect to their future relations in that area.

II. The political and economic conditions which have contributed to the present course of Japanese foreign policy and possible important future developments; the extent to which Japan's policy toward China has been influenced by Japan's geographic conditions and material resources, by special features in the political and economic organization of Japan which directly or indirectly affect the formulation of her present foreign policy, by economic and political developments in China, by the external policies of other Powers affecting Japan; the principal political, economic and social factors which may be expected in a post-war Japan; possible and probable adjustments on the part of other nations which could aid in the solution of Japan's fundamental problems.

III. The political and economic conditions which have contributed to the present course of Chinese foreign policy and possible important future developments; Chinese unification and reconstruction, 1931-37, and steps leading toward the policy of united national resistance to Japan; the present degree of political cohesion and economic strength; effects of resistance and current developments on the position of foreign interests in China and changes in China's relations with foreign Powers; the principal political, economic and social factors which may be expected in a post-war China; possible and probable adjustments on the part of other nations which could aid in the solution of China's fundamental problems.

IV. Possible methods for the adjustment of specific problems, in the light of information and suggestions presented in the three studies outlined above; analysis of previous attempts at bilateral or multilateral adjustments of political and economic relations in the Pacific and causes of their success or failure; types of administrative procedures and controls already tried out and their relative effectiveness; the major issues likely to require international adjustment in a post-war period and the most hopeful methods which might be devised to meet them; necessary adjustments by the Powers concerned; the basic requirements of a practical system of international organization which could promote the security and peaceful development of the countries of the Pacific area.

EDWARD C. CARTER
Secretary-General

*New York,
September 2, 1940*

AUTHOR'S PREFACE

Economic questions such as standards of living, availability of raw materials, competitive ability of industries, and trade restrictions will be very important when the time comes for a bilateral or multilateral peace settlement in the Far East. Nevertheless, a peace treaty is a political agreement and even more dependent on intangibles like security, confidence, and public opinion. Consequently, sound peace negotiations may easily be jeopardized by emotional biases such as have been encouraged during recent years by the repeated charges of "fascism," "totalitarianism," "militarism," and "feudalism" made in discussions of Japanese political trends. A new interpretation of those political trends may, therefore, claim a legitimate place in the documentation for discussions of the problem of a peace settlement.

It is the author's considered opinion that these epithets, at least in the derogatory sense in which they are usually applied, are dangerously misleading and that their use is due to lack of perspective. They are superficial judgments on political tendencies which, in reality, have origins far beyond the present crisis and are but Japanese counterparts of trends evident throughout the world, including the United States, France, and the British Empire. This is an interpretation and, as such, is not susceptible to formal proof in the same sense that we can establish facts regarding trade expansion or wage levels. If this paper makes evident the *possibility* of an explanation of Japanese political trends which is less sensational than that generally current, it will have served its purpose.

Responsibility for this interpretation cannot be shifted from the author's shoulders to those of other scholars. Accordingly, footnotes have been included primarily for the convenience of readers wishing guidance toward documentary sources and interesting collateral discussions otherwise difficult to locate.

A desire to utilize the limited space available for emphasis on trends and international parallels has compelled the omission of many details of recent political history. For these, as well as for somewhat different general interpretations, the reader may wish to consult other Inquiry studies being issued by the Secretariat of the Institute of Pacific Relations. Those in preparation include *Political and Social Developments in Japan Since 1931* by Dr. Hugh Borton, *The Political Significance of the Japanese Army* by Dr. Kenneth W. Colegrove, and *Agriculture and Population Problems in Japan* by Miss Miriam S. Farley. The development of economic control in the early Meiji period has been referred to only briefly in the present study; a more complete discussion will be found in Mr. E. H. Norman's *Japan's Emergence as a Modern State*. Parts of the present study, notably the materials on guilds, overlap the contents of Miss Farley's *The Problem of Japanese Trade Expansion in the Post-War Situation* and Professor G. C. Allen's *Japanese Industry: Its Recent Development and Present Condition*. The points of view of the latter studies are, however, primarily economic. They are interested in the war-time development of Japan's foreign trade and industry respectively. The present study, on the other hand, is concerned with the guilds from a political standpoint, with their role in the trend toward greater state control of economic life. This accounts for some other differences as well, e.g., minimization of the influence of the war. No doubt the war has accelerated the development of economic control. From an economic point of view it has also shifted the emphasis of that control, i.e., from light to heavy industry. From the political point of view, however, the shift has been much smaller. Government control is government control whether directed toward an increase in cotton exports or toward a rise in steel production, and the trend toward such control antedates even the Manchurian incident.

The reader must also look elsewhere for detailed evaluations of the *accomplishments* under recent Japanese legislation. It would be physically impossible for one student to make such detailed estimates of the administration of hundreds of measures, and there are few monographs on which one can rely. Moreover, this study is more interested in what the Japanese are *trying* to do, and why, than in the degree of success of their efforts; the wisdom of their laws and the efficiency of their administrators will be tested well enough by the war. This, of course, does not mean that the author assumes that control is accomplished as soon as a statute authorizing it is passed by the Diet: Japan like every other nation has a liberal quota of still-born legislation.

There is a genuine need for more specialized monographs on

single phases of modern Japanese politics or economics such as election reform, reorganization of army leadership, health insurance, or any one of the numerous "national policy corporations." Until we have many studies on such subjects which show not only the Japanese origins of specific policies but also Western precedents and parallels, it will be impossible to prepare any summary of recent Japanese trends which is both balanced and thoroughly reliable. Such summaries are an essential foundation for intelligent lay thinking on Western relations with Japan. Yet the scarcity of Western scholars who know Japanese and the paucity of most American and European library resources on modern Japanese developments give little hope for an early supply of the necessary foundation. The present study is offered, in full recognition of its inadequacies, only as an emergency antidote to sensational journalism.

C. B. F.

March, 1940.

NOTE

Japanese personal names in this work are given in the conventional Japanese form, that is the family name preceding the given name, except in cases such as Prince T. Iwakura or Sterling Tatsuji Takeuchi which cannot satisfactorily be rendered except in an order adapted to Western usage.

CONTENTS

FOREWORD vii
AUTHOR'S PREFACE xi
INTRODUCTION 3

PART I. EXPANSION OF GOVERNMENTAL RESPONSIBILITIES

  1. Promotion and Regulation of Foreign Trade . . 9
  2. Economic Recovery and Security 24
  3. Overseas Development and Domestic Control . . 37
  4. National Defense 44
  5. Social Welfare 53
  6. Finance 57

PART II. POLITICAL AND ADMINISTRATIVE REORGANIZATION

  1. Administrative Problems 63
  2. Legislature and Executive 71
  3. Education, Information and Propaganda . . . 81

PART III. CONCLUSIONS 88
BIBLIOGRAPHICAL NOTE 90
INDEX 101
LIST OF STATUTES CITED 111

GOVERNMENT IN JAPAN

RECENT TRENDS IN ITS SCOPE AND OPERATION

INTRODUCTION

Despite certain differences in the surface manifestations of national life—differences which have too often monopolized the attention of Western observers—Japanese political developments during the last seventy years have closely followed Western paths. This has meant, in Japan as elsewhere, a steady advance toward more pervasive regulation by the government of the activities of its individual citizens. This tendency is everywhere as old as politics itself but was manifested with new insistence toward the middle of the last century in expanding municipal functions such as police, sanitation, water supply, street lighting, and the rudiments of labor legislation. The process was vastly speeded up during the World War and has continued unabated ever since until today the multiplication of government services, new functions, and new problems is compelling in each country serious consideration of plans for political reorganization to meet new conditions.

Japan joined the family of nations when this new stage in an old parade was just getting well under way. She swung into line almost immediately. The new government enacted quarantine and sanitary laws, established municipal services, granted licenses, and appointed police inspectors. There were some original Japanese variations, like police supervision of annual house-cleaning, but, on the whole, Japan followed Western innovations almost too closely. Fortunately Japanese statesmen were wise enough to consult more than one teacher and to choose with discrimination some political methods from the United States, some from England, France, Switzerland or Holland, and others from Germany. The final synthesis preserved a few indigenous institutions and was better suited to Japanese problems under new conditions than any less eclectic product could have been. In subsequent years industry and governmental regulation advanced in Japan in much the same direction as they did in the West. No two countries are identical in background or development, however, and in Japan a number of conditions modified the details of the evolution. A brief statement of the most important of these will help to clarify more recent events.

1. Japanese recognized economic regulation as a legitimate

function, even an obligation, of the government. The Tokugawa shogunate had licensed and regulated business in Edo and Osaka, sometimes constructively, sometimes by futile sumptuary laws. It had also undertaken extensive public works. The most respected provincial lords were those who carried out reclamation and riparian works and promoted special industries.[1] Had Japan come on the international scene a few years earlier, these habits might have been overcome by the authority of Western liberal economics. But in the 1870's continental economic thinkers, both socialist and nationalist, were already urging government regulation and even ownership of industry. So in following the West, Japan did not feel obligated to discontinue official economic guidance.

2. Japanese merchants were accustomed to co-operative organization and self-regulation through a guild system (*kabunakama*) developed partly in self-defense and partly at the instigation of the shogunate officials. Although the power of the *kabunakama* was broken even before the Restoration, the usefulness of such organizations was not forgotten and was recognized once more in the 1880's in legislation permitting the organization of occupational associations under statutory restrictions and a new name—*kumiai*. The *kumiai* steadily expanded in numbers and strength. As well-tried instruments for the application of a judicious mixture of legislative guidance and self-control, they have obviated some of the acrimony between government and business which has developed in other countries. The restrictions placed on American trade associations, for instance, by the Sherman Anti-trust Law would be out of place and unwanted in Japan.

3. The critical position, both political and economic, in which Restoration Japan found herself led to early, frequent and far-reaching governmental guidance of industrial development which set a precedent for later years. Japan had seen China twice attacked and beaten by European powers, and there were intrigues enough to warn her of a similar fate. Obviously her need for arsenals, iron foundries, and shipyards was too urgent to await their slow development by individual initiative: the government built them itself. The telegraph was recognized as of military importance and was made a government

---

[1] English accounts of economic policies of the Tokugawa regime are given in Takekoshi Yosaburo, *The Economic Aspects of the History of the Civilization of Japan*, New York, 1930, Vols. II and III, and in Honjo Eijiro, *The Social and Economic History of Japan*, Tokyo, 1935.

monopoly as in France and other continental countries. The government took the lead in railway building from the beginning—a policy wisely calculated to avoid political abuse of foreign investments such as subsequently developed in China. General economic strength in non-military fields was equally important, however, and Japan's small-scale handicraft industries were vulnerable to competition from European and American machine-made products. Exchange provisions in the early treaties led to depletion of Japan's metallic currency, while unilateral treaty restrictions on tariffs prevented indirect fostering of young industries. Adopting the sole alternative of direct encouragement, the government built model factories, hired foreign experts, forced improvements in quality by compulsory inspection, and handed out subsidies to the limit which a depleted treasury permitted. The medicine helped the patient and has since been prescribed again from time to time as occasion warranted. A by-product was the promotion of near monopolies and trusts. The object was to establish economic institutions able to compete with the West on equal terms and there was neither time nor money to waste on weaklings. Strong firms were helped to become stronger; in later years cartels and trusts were encouraged. Japan could not afford anti-trust legislation like the Sherman and Clayton Acts in the United States. She preferred harnessing big business enterprises to prosecuting them.[2]

4. The Japanese Constitution is flexible: in neither wording nor interpretation does it contain restrictions on effective economic control. In the first place, while very difficult to amend, the Japanese Constitution is very adaptable; it merely outlines the essentials of the governmental structure and leaves the details to ordinary legislation. The twelfth, sixteenth, seventeenth, eighteenth, nineteenth, twentieth, and twenty-first amendments to the American Constitution would not have been necessary in Japan. Changes affecting income taxes, prohibition, or woman suffrage all have been or could be adopted by ordinary law or ordinance.

Secondly, the Constitution makes Japan, like England or France, a centralized state. The national government has plenary powers, the prefectures only those powers delegated to them. Thus the Japanese Government can regulate production

[2] A recent outline of government industrial policy in the early Meiji period appears in E. H. Norman, *Japan's Emergence as a Modern State*, I.P.R. Inquiry Series, New York, 1940, Chapter II.

directly without resorting to the subterfuge of controlling interstate commerce as has had to be done in the United States. The courts do not presume to declare unconstitutional laws which the Emperor and the Diet have approved; but even if they did, there would be no danger of a major national economic recovery measure being invalidated because of its application not being restricted to interstate commerce.

Thirdly, the Japanese Constitution does not place narrow limits around the delegation of rule-making authority to executive organs. In fact, the Japanese Constitution specifically recognizes wide ordinance powers and it is customary for the Japanese Diet, like the British Parliament, to devote its limited time and energies to the essential outlines of legislative measures, leaving the details to be drafted and promulgated by competent technicians in the administrative civil service.

Finally, while the Japanese Constitution contains an article closely resembling the American due-process clause, this article is interpreted in the original English sense. It protects the citizen against arbitrary and illegal acts of administrative officers but not against curtailment of his property rights by laws enacted in the public interest after due consideration by the Diet, the cabinet, and the Emperor. It cannot be invoked to nullify labor legislation or to escape rate regulation as the due-process clause has so frequently been employed before the American courts.

Japan has thus been psychologically and socially prepared for economic control, has been impelled toward it by political and economic pressure, and has had a constitution permitting it. Nevertheless, until a few years ago the desires of her businessmen and a widespread respect for classical economic liberalism led her to continue to allow very wide scope for individual initiative and free competition. Since the World War, however, several factors of world-wide character have impelled her toward the greater economic control which her institutions permit. The two most important of these can be stated briefly.

1. Throughout the world there is increasing reluctance to accept economic law as inexorable, increasing demand from all sides, including business, that governments do something about one or another economic situation. One need not go to Japan to discover some of the reasons for this: there is a certain incongruity between universal conscription and economic *laissez faire*; the World War provided widespread practice in

economic control and it seemed logical that methods used to defeat the enemy might also help to beat the depression; the primary and secondary post-War depressions were peculiarly severe and their causes were so distant from the local scene that rugged individualism seemed an inadequate solution; socialist theory and the example of the Soviet Union contributed to the same dissatisfaction with *laissez faire*.

Imports succumbed to regulation first because on questions of foreign trade one of the interested parties had no voice in national elections. Thus tariffs mounted and were supplemented by quotas and embargoes. Since these were applied primarily against manufactured articles, they affected most seriously those nations poor in raw materials and in controlled markets and contributed to their currency difficulties caused by abnormal post-War financing. Exchange restrictions and barter agreements became the only alternatives to uncontrolled inflation but interfered further with free private movement of goods. Protectionism also compelled the adoption of extraordinary promotional measures by exporting nations. Controls multiplied.

The depression of the past decade brought with it demands for government steps in the interest of economic recovery and stability, or, as the Japanese phrase runs, stabilization of the national livelihood. Control and regulation thus turned inward, as was inevitable in any case, for control of foreign trade could scarcely help but lead to control of production at home.

At the same time demands for social legislation—better working conditions, minimum wages, maximum hours, unemployment insurance, health insurance, old age insurance—created additional, almost irresistible pressure for further governmental regulation and control of all phases of economic life.

2. The World War had a second major consequence: it underlined in unforgettable fashion the increasing importance of economic and psychological factors in war. Germany's long resistance was made possible by the genius of her scientists and by the amazing organization of her industry. Her defeat was economic rather than military in any narrow sense. The World War made mineral surveys, chemical laboratories, and factories the daily preoccupation of general staffs in all countries. Mobilization plans in each major country have come to include schedules for the integration of the whole productive machinery of the nation. Where essential minerals or manufactured

products are inadequate, substitute materials are sought or new industries promoted. Even the wealthiest nations have added some measures of economic control to their national defense preparations.

Control of opinion has similarly gained in importance because of World War experience. The effective Allied propaganda campaign and its role in hastening the German collapse has, like economic mobilization, been studied by all general staffs. It is obvious that with military power dependent on the total mobilization of the productive forces of the country, much depends on public morale. Realization of this fact leads not only to military support for reform measures tending to minimize social discontent but also to serious concern over the development in peace as well as in war of currents of thought which weaken national unity. These characteristics of modern war, which were effectively demonstrated from 1914 to 1918, have forced every nation toward a greater measure of direction of both the economic activities and the emotions and thoughts of its citizens.

These trends toward broader governmental activity are international in character. They can be traced in every country which has a modern national defense organization and anything more than a rudimentary industrial system. They know no ideological boundaries although their manifestations vary with the economic, social, intellectual, and legal resources of individual countries.

The first purpose of this study is to show how these various trends have developed in Japan during the last few years under the special conditions of that country. It will then be possible to describe reforms and proposed reforms in the political and administrative machinery of the country in proper relation to the new and complex functions of government which have impelled them. Only when this has been done can we view Japan's internal development with some degree of perspective both as to its relations to developments in other parts of the world and as to its connection, either as cause or effect, with Japanese expansion on the continent of Asia.

Obviously such a broad field can be covered only in outline. No attempt is made to analyze individual statutes or reforms in detail or to assess their exact economic results, nor is any judgment attempted or implied as to the morality or legality of Japanese actions on the continent of Asia.

PART I
EXPANSION OF GOVERNMENTAL RESPONSIBILITIES

The motives for expansion of governmental responsibilities and activities are numerous, complex, and interrelated. Were this not the case the trend would be neither so ubiquitous nor so persistent. Consequently no new policy can be attributed exclusively to a single motive. There were, for example, a great many arguments for the entrance by the United States government into power development first at Muscle Shoals and subsequently elsewhere in the Tennessee Valley: curtailment of American dependence on imports of Chilean guano; elevation of living standards in a depressed area; aid to national economic recovery through increased purchasing power; farm relief through provision of cheap fertilizers; experimentation in social and economic reform; creation of a measuring stick for private utility rates; augmentation of the potential supply of nitrates for military use; increase of power resources available for industrial mobilization in time of war; improvement of navigable waterways. Japanese leaders, whether trained in the army, the civil services or in private business, are no more single-minded than American congressmen; their policies also have many facets. Nevertheless, it is convenient here to classify recent enactments under the following headings according to the motives which seem to have been most influential in their adoption:

Promotion and regulation of foreign trade.
Economic recovery and security.
Integration of overseas development and domestic control.
National defense.
Social reform.
Finance.

1. PROMOTION AND REGULATION OF FOREIGN TRADE

Prior to the World War Japan's foreign trade policy was thoroughly orthodox and consisted of a small degree of protection through customs tariffs, enforcement of the grading and inspection of export commodities, encouragement to shipping, state aid to trade fairs, sample museums, and participation in international expositions.

The War-time boom was welcome and uncontrolled, but the post-War decade was a peculiarly serious one for Japan. Many of the industrial and export advances made under abnormal war conditions were not sufficiently established to withstand renewed European competition and the loss of special war markets. As in other parts of the world, prices and debt structures had become inflated. Moreover, Japan enjoyed no real boom between the primary and secondary post-War depressions. The great earthquake occurred just when world recovery was under way, and the strain of reconstruction weakened innumerable Japanese financial and business institutions, seriously unbalanced foreign trade, and threatened currency stability. Reconstruction was still incomplete when the Bank of Taiwan closed its doors in 1927, precipitating a major financial panic which was checked only by strenuous governmental measures. When the Minseito Cabinet two years later sought rehabilitation through a painful program of deflation and the re-establishment of the gold standard at the old yen parity, its plans were upset by the 1929 crash, the collapse of the American silk market, and the devaluation of the pound sterling. As a result of this prolonged depression, the Japanese government was impelled during the decade prior to 1931 toward emergency measures much as was the government of the United States somewhat later, but Japan's greater dependence on foreign trade precluded the belief in recovery through internal measures alone which has characterized much recent American legislation. Promotion of foreign trade was inevitably a major part of any Japanese recovery program.

In this program tariffs have played a minor role, for Japan's tariff policy has always been moderate.[1] It was compelled to be moderate for many years after the Restoration since the five per cent tariff imposed by the unequal treaties provided little revenue and less protection. It was natural that Japan should raise her tariffs in 1899 and 1911 as these restrictions were thrown off, but the increases were limited by Japan's dependence on imported raw materials and her need to keep the food prices for the working population within bounds. Like most

[1] For a general summary of Japanese tariff policy and for tables showing the average rate of customs duties through 1928, see Tominaga Yugi, "Nippon Kanzei Seisaku" (Japanese Tariff Policy), *Keizaigaku Jiten* (Dictionary of Economics), Vol. IV, pp. 2002-5.

Western countries, Japan adopted anti-dumping duties after the World War and raised some schedules to protect new industries which had flourished under war conditions. The 1926 tariff revision did little more than consolidate these changes. The last general revision, in 1932, was made necessary by price fluctuations and the re-imposition of the gold embargo. Together with subsequent amendments, it provides added protection in many lines but is, on the average, relatively liberal even if not as close to free trade as some economists advocate. Instead of prohibitive tariffs, which are clumsy and inadequate tools for a country heavily dependent on foreign trade, Japan has sought more flexible and effective instruments of regulation in trade associations, exchange control, and semi-official corporate monopolies.

Trade Associations

Trade associations, which have a long tradition in Japan,[2] were given legal recognition in the Standard Rules for Joint Occupation Associations (*Dogyo Kumiai Junsoku*) promulgated by the Department of Agriculture and Commerce in 1884, by the Staple Exports Guilds Law (*Juyo Yushutsu Hin Dogyo Kumiai Ho*) of 1897, and by the Staple Commodities Guilds Law (*Juyo Bussan Dogyo Kumiai Ho*) of 1900.[3] The principal objectives of these early statutes and associations were the inspection and standardization of export commodities—measures necessary to foster development of overseas markets[4]—and for these purposes the government gave the associations some degree of legal support. The 1900 statute, for example, made membership in a guild compulsory under certain circumstances. Price agreements were, on the other hand, prohibited in 1917 by the Vice-Minister of Agriculture and Commerce.

Both private businessmen and public officials saw in the strengthening and multiplication of the guilds a possible means

[2] The article on "Guilds" in the *Encyclopaedia of the Social Sciences* contains a section on Japan by G. C. Allen which gives a brief and useful summary of the early history of the guilds. See also Ogata Kiyoshi, *The Co-operative Movement in Japan*. London, 1923.

[3] See Kishi Shinsuke, "Juyo Bussan Dogyo Kumiai" (Staple Commodities Guilds), in *Horitsugaku Jiten* (Dictionary of Jurisprudence), II, pp. 1246-8.

[4] The issuance of the Standard Rules was directly related to the application by the United States in 1883 of regulations to check importation of low-grade tea. See Takahashi Kamekichi, *Nippon Tosei Keizai Ron* (Japanese Economic Control), p. 166.

of combating trade stagnation.[5] In 1925 the coalition party cabinet of Kato Taka-akira enacted the Staple Exports Industrial Guilds Law (*Juyo Yushutsu Hin Kogyo Kumiai Ho*) and the Export Guilds Law (*Yushutsu Kumiai Ho*) which between them authorized it to strengthen both private and public control of manufacture for export and the export business itself.[6] Under these laws guilds of the two types were encouraged to undertake such additional joint enterprises as overseas representation and marketing, investigation and promotion of markets, co-operative purchasing of raw materials, and co-operative establishments for inspecting, sorting, grading, wrapping, and packing. In return, their agreements were made subject to ministerial approval. National financial aid for some of the joint undertakings of the guilds and their control of inspection facilities helped to make membership obligatory in fact if not in law. In 1931 the Export Guilds Law and the Industrial Guilds Law were further amended to give the guilds financial powers—to enable them to accept deposits by members, to make loans for productive purposes, and to finance exports. They were also authorized to fix rules for the time, areas, quantities, and prices of exports. The appropriate minister of state was given authority, when necessary for the development of trade or the protection of national interests, to enforce guild agreements even against outsiders.[7] The ability of the guilds to control foreign trade on a rational basis was thus greatly increased while the government was given additional powers of regulation in the national interest.[8]

[5] The 1925 measures were carried in the House of Representatives *unanimously*. *Tokyo Asahi*, February 18, 1925, 18-3. (In all references to the *Tokyo Asahi* in this study the dating and pagination of the *shukusatsuban*, or monthly reduced-size edition, will be used.)

[6] A summary of the 1925 statute is given in the *Tokyo Asahi*, February 1, 1925, 1-7. The Japanese texts of the *Yushutsu Kumiai Ho* as amended in 1931 and of the rules for its application are given in Appendices 1 and 2 in Taniguchi Kichihiko, *Boeki Tosei Ron* (Trade Control), Tokyo, 1934.

[7] The 1931 amendments are summarized in the *Tokyo Asahi*, January 10, 1931, 10-1.

[8] Japanese legislation is not unrelated to the United States Webb-Pomerene Export Trade Act of 1918 which exempts export associations from the restrictions of the anti-trust laws. Japan has, however, strengthened her export associations further than has the United States, and has depended on discretionary administrative supervision rather than on statutory prescriptions for the prevention of abuses. Compare also the Export Control Boards established in New Zealand following the World War (1921-5).

The guilds and the legislation controlling them have been put to a new use since 1931—to facilitate Japanese compliance with Western demands for control of the tempo of her export boom. The rapid increase of Japanese exports after 1932 was particularly resented abroad because it added to the difficulties of businesses already suffering from the depression. Special tariff schedules, quotas, and embargoes against Japanese goods or threats of similar discriminatory action were reported every few days during 1933 and 1934 from every continent and almost every country or colony. Such measures were defended on relatively new grounds. Ostensibly it was not the Japanese export advance per se which was considered objectionable, but its disturbing speed and disproportionately low prices; the latter were popularly attributed to "exchange dumping" or "social dumping." Japan sought to forestall these new threats to the improvement of her living standards by offering to control more effectively both the volume and the prices of her exports. For this purpose the mandatory provisions of the Export Guilds Law were invoked.[9] Examples are numerous. Early in 1934 the Minister of Commerce and Industry urged exporters of electric bulbs and matches to the United States to organize for price control; in April 1934 silk and rayon textile exporters decided to inaugurate price control; in May 1935 plans were announced for the organization of an export guild to control quantities and prices of cotton yarn and textile exports to Africa; in June 1935 the Minister of Commerce and Industry instructed the Japan Knitted Goods Export Guild to enforce stricter control of quantities and prices of commodities sent to the Dutch East Indies, British North Borneo, the Straits Settlements, and New Guinea; in August 1936 ceramic exports were ordered controlled over a wide area; in January 1936 stricter control of cotton export prices was reported; compulsory provisions were applied to rayon exports in September 1936.

Quantitative limitations were sometimes applied as purely preventive measures, and sometimes as a result of negotiated agreements, private or diplomatic. For example, in January 1934 the organization of Japanese nitrate producers signed an agreement with the European nitrogen cartel regarding exports of ammonium sulphate (renewed in November 1935); in April

[9] Trade control through the guilds is well explained in Taniguchi Kichihiko, *Boeki Tosei Ron*, pp. 207-36.

1934 the Federation of Pencil Exporters' Associations decided to restrict exports to the United States to 125,000 gross per quarter; in May 1934 British and Japanese traders signed an agreement in London, placing a quota on exports of Japanese electric bulbs to Britain; in October 1935 the United States Department of State announced a two-year gentlemen's agreement governing limitation of Japanese cotton textile exports to the Philippine Islands (extended for one year in July 1938). Such limitations on quantities had even more far-reaching effects than those on prices, for they compelled the allocation of orders among exporting firms and, eventually, the inauguration of factory production quotas. It is worth noting once more that such restrictions would have been extremely difficult to apply had it not been for the strongly established guild system. Needless to say, it was foreign pressure, not a Japanese love for regulation, which made them necessary.

A further development of control was required to meet widespread insistence outside of Japan that she balance her bilateral trade with specific countries, or to utilize Japanese purchases abroad in bargaining for trade concessions. The connection is shown in many trade disputes, conferences and agreements between 1933 and 1939. A Turco-Japanese trade equalization agreement was signed at Ankara on July 26, 1934 as a result of a Turkish ruling in the previous year that Japan must buy from Turkey at least fifty per cent of the amount sold there. In June 1935 Japan proposed that her merchants purchase enough Cuban sugar and tobacco to exempt Japanese goods from the double tariff imposed by Cuba on imports from nations purchasing less than twenty-five per cent of the value of the goods sold in Cuba. An agreement between the Japan to Africa and the Near East Export Guild and the government of Syria for the purchase of Syrian products to balance Japanese sales was reported in August 1936. The latest revision of this arrangement with Syria, an official treaty also on the barter principle, was signed in July 1939.[10] Negotiations for similar agreements with other small countries have frequently been necessary but more important were those with India, the Dutch East Indies, Australia, Canada, Burma, Germany, and Italy.[11]

[10] *Trans-Pacific*, August 10, 1939, p. 17.
[11] For a general discussion of recent agreements and the problems involved see "Japan's Recent Trade Agreements," *Oriental Economist*, Vol. VI, September 1939, pp. 589-92.

The Indo-Japanese agreement, signed after much delay on July 12, 1934, made the amount of Japanese cotton goods admitted to India at a non-prohibitory duty dependent on the amount of Indian raw cotton purchased by Japan in an earlier but overlapping period. The March 1937 agreement with Burma was similar except that Japan undertook to purchase sixty-five per cent of all Burmese cotton available for export in return for a fixed import quota.[12] These agreements placed the burden of control almost entirely on Japan and were workable only because of Japanese legislation. The Indian agreement, for example, resulted first in the issuance on January 7, 1934 of an order by the Department of Commerce and Industry requiring certification of all cotton goods exports to India (*Menorimono Indo Yushutsu Shomei Kisoku*), and second in the organization on March 1, 1934 of the Japan to India Cotton Goods Export Association (*Nippon Menorimono Tai Indo Yushutsu Kumiai*) which was to assume the necessary duties of control.[13] In view of Anglo-Saxon insistence on the beauties of free trade and the reasonableness of the present distribution of resources, it is interesting that British colonial policies should have thus forced Japan into assumption of inconvenient state restrictions which possession of the colonies permits Britain to escape or postpone.

The more complex trade dispute with the Dutch East Indies led to mobilization of many groups in order to apply bargaining pressure and to facilitate equitable operation of the resultant quotas: Japanese retailers in Java were organized, the Japanese shipping lines operating services to the Dutch East Indies were consolidated, Japanese exporters of ceramics and cotton goods enforced first boycotts and then quotas.[14] Effective negotiation with Australia required co-operation not only between shipping lines and cotton exporters, but also between importers of wool and manufacturers of woolen goods. The effects spread when Manchukuo agreed to co-operate in retaliation against Australian products. Even shippers to Africa were brought in. Both to secure substitute supplies and as part

[12] See C. N. Vakil and D. N. Maluste, *Commercial Relations between India and Japan*, London, 1937, pp. 177-206.
[13] On the Indo-Japanese agreement see Taniguchi Kichihiko, *Boeki Tosei Ron* (Trade Control), pp. 140-56. Also, Ogata Hanshi, "Nichi-In Boeki Mondai" (the Indo-Japanese Trade Problem), *Keizaigaku Jiten*, Supplement, pp. 409-11.
[14] See Miriam S. Farley, "Dutch-Japanese Negotiations Resumed," *Far Eastern Survey*, IV, 16, August 14, 1935, pp. 129-30.

of a plan to forestall new restrictions on Japanese imports by the Union of South Africa, Japanese exporters taxed themselves in order to raise funds to subsidize Japanese wool purchases from that area.[15]

The 1935 trade dispute with Canada as well as that of 1936 with Australia led to application of a new statute, the Trade Protection Law (*Boeki Chosetsu oyobi Tsusho Yogo ni Kansuru Horitsu*) which permitted the application of retaliatory tariffs.[16]

The new barter agreements with Germany and Italy required, strangely enough, less control on the Japanese side than those with so-called "liberal" countries because the co-signers were able and willing to assume their share of the burden. The agreement between Manchukuo and Germany of April 30, 1936 (renewed in May 1937 and revised on September 14, 1938)[17] was really triangular in nature and was enforced by means of blocked marks and special accounts in Germany.[18] That between Italy, Manchukuo, and Japan of July 5, 1938 is controlled by special accounts on each side.[19] Both these agreements, however, necessitated the imposition of a license system on private trade deals.

The latest agreement with Australia, announced late in June

[15] See "Pool for Buying South African Wool," *Oriental Economist*, II, 12, December 1935, pp. 14-16; "Boycotting Australian Wool," *ibid.*, III, 7, July 1936, pp. 420-1; "Japan's Wool Supply and the Dispute with Australia," *Far Eastern Survey*, V, 16, July 29, 1936, pp. 172-3. The dispute with Australia was settled by a barter arrangement embodied in notes exchanged on December 26, 1936, and printed in *Contemporary Japan*, V, 4, March 1937, pp. 700-3.

[16] The Japanese text of the Trade Protection Law is given in Supplement 3 to Taniguchi Kichihiko, *Boeki Tosei Ron* (Trade Control). The settlement of the dispute with Canada was embodied in notes exchanged on December 25, 1935 and printed in *Contemporary Japan*, IV, 4, March 1936, pp. 633-5.

[17] See *Oriental Economist*, III, 6, June 1936, p. 344, and Kurt Bloch, "German-Japanese Partnership in Eastern Asia," *Far Eastern Survey*, VII, 21, October 26, 1938, pp. 241-5. An unofficial translation of the text of the 1938 agreement is given in the *Japan-Manchoukuo Year Book*, *1939*, pp. 857-8.

[18] A provisional trade agreement between Japan and Germany was signed on July 29, 1939, but its terms have not yet been published. It is reported to have provided for balancing of the trade between Germany and Japan-Manchukuo on a one-to-one basis. See "Japanese-German Trade Pact," *Oriental Economist*, VI, 9, September 1939, pp. 594-6.

[19] See unofficial translation of text in the *Manchuria Daily News*, August 28, 1938, pp. 1, 8. See also *Oriental Economist*, V, 6, June 1938, p. 407; *Trans-Pacific*, July 14, 1938, p. 4. That such agreements had little to do with the Anti-Comintern Pact is suggested by the fact that New Zealand negotiated an analogous reciprocal trade agreement with Germany in October 1937. See W. B. Sutch, "The Ottawa Agreement and After," *Economic Record* (Melbourne), Vol. XV, October 1939, Supplement, p. 44.

1939, introduced a new element: Japan agreed to purchase two-thirds of her total wool imports from Australia while continuing a voluntary restriction of 51,250,000 square yards per year on textile exports.[20] The definite ratio of purchases is made possible, however, only by the licensing of imports, which requires an explanation of the use of exchange control as related to foreign trade.

Exchange Control

Exchange control for trade promotion and regulation may be said to begin with such measures as devaluation and the establishment of exchange stabilization funds, operative in Japan as well as in Great Britain and the United States. Yet these, like tariffs, are scarcely adequate under critical circumstances. Japan's lack of resources and capital places her in a weaker commercial and financial position than the United States and has necessitated more incisive measures to check the flight of capital and to permit the maintenance of a stable currency in the face of budgetary deficits and a passive foreign trade produced both by trade restrictions abroad and an armaments boom at home.

A Capital Flight Prevention Law (*Shihon Tohi Boshi Ho*) was enacted in the summer of 1932, a few months after the reimposition of the embargo on gold exports. Under this law, bank reports on exchange transactions became compulsory. This act was soon replaced by the much stronger Foreign Exchange Control Law (*Gaikoku Kawase Kanri Ho*), adopted by the Diet in March 1933, which is the basis for most subsequent orders in regard to exchange.[21] The Foreign Exchange Control Law permits, but does not compel, the government to prohibit or limit the acquisition and disposal of securities and debentures in foreign currencies, the issue and acquisition of letters of credit, the granting of credits to persons resident abroad, the import and export of securities, and the export of articles the price of which is wholly or in part not covered by foreign exchange. It authorizes the government to concentrate foreign

[20] *Trans-Pacific*, July 6, 1939, p. 40.
[21] See an English translation of the text in W. J. Sebald, *A Selection of Japan's Emergency Legislation*, Kobe, 1937, pp. 1-5. For discussion see Kimpara Kennosuke, "Kawase Kanri" (Exchange Control), *Keizaigaku Jiten*, Supplement, pp. 79-81. Also Aoki Ichio, "Gaikoku Kawase Kanri Ho," (Foreign Exchange Control Law), *Horitsugaku Jiten*, Vol. I, pp. 164-5.

exchange transactions in the Bank of Japan or in other specified banks and to require the compulsory sale to the government of exchange, securities, or currency at prices fixed by a Foreign Currency Valuation Commission (*Gaika Hyoka Iinkai*). A Foreign Exchange Control Commission (*Gaikoku Kawase Kanri Iinkai*) was established to advise the government on the application of the act. This law was strengthened by amendment in September 1937 to facilitate requisitioning of property held or payable abroad.[22]

The Exchange Control Law was not invoked to any considerable degree until January 8, 1937. Although this was prior to the Lukouchiao incident, the import excess was already alarming, and export of gold to maintain the yen was imminent. On that date, exchange settlements in payment for imports when amounting to more than ¥30,000 per month were made subject to license.[23] This limit of exemption from control has been progressively lowered by new enforcement ordinances—to ¥1,000 on July 7, 1937 and to ¥100 in December 1937. Similar restrictions on credits for Japanese travellers abroad and remittances to residents in other countries were imposed and progressively tightened. From July 1937 reports on all exports and the exchange covering them and licenses for exports not covered by foreign exchange were required. In December 1937, under Diet amendments to the Exchange Control Law, disposal or hypothecation of Japanese property abroad was put under license, and reports on property held and business conducted abroad were made compulsory. Although this one act thus made possible trenchant governmental regulation of foreign exchange, further measures were enforced following the outbreak of hostilities in China.

The first of these, the Law Concerning Adjustment of Foreign Trade and Industries Related Thereto (*Boeki oyobi Kankei Sangyo no Chosei ni Kansuru Horitsu*), was adopted by the 71st Diet, which met in August 1937 but had been sum-

---

[22] For the text of the enforcement order and discussion see *Tokyo Asahi*, January 8, 1937, p. 98; January 10, 1937, p. 134. See also Elizabeth Boody, "Manchukuo, the Key to Japan's Foreign Exchange Problem," *Far Eastern Survey*, VI, 10, May 12, 1937, pp. 107-12; "Politics and the Yen," *ibid.*, VI, 11, May 26, 1937, pp. 117-22.

[23] The Japanese text of the amendment is given in the *Tokyo Asahi*, September 5, 1937, p. 70. See also *ibid.*, December 7, 1937, p. 102; December 10, 1937, p. 148.

moned prior to the Lukouchiao incident. This law authorized the government to restrict or prohibit imports or exports for the purpose of carrying out treaties, adjusting international payments, reforming trade treaties, or assuring a healthy development of the national economy.[24] A Trade Council (*Boeki Shingi-kai*) was established to advise on such restrictions prior to their adoption. A Control Consultation Board (*Tosei Kyogi-kai*) composed of businessmen was also authorized to facilitate the adjustments of private interests which applications of the law might require.[25] Control of exports and imports was broadened and extended to domestic distribution and use by the Emergency Imports Exports Management Law (*Yushutsunyu Rinji Sochi Ho*), passed by the special 72nd Diet in September 1937.[26] It was applied in October by a departmental ordinance prohibiting importation of some 231 commodities and has also provided legal foundation for the compulsory monopolization under special corporations of the distribution of key commodities, e.g., iron and copper scrap.[27] Reports on exchange transactions in excess of 500 yen in invisible trade were made compulsory by a Department of Finance regulation promulgated in April 1938 under the Emergency Capital Adjustment Law (*Rinji Shikin Chosei Ho*).[28]

This drastic control of imports during the first months of the China incident was applied without adequate consideration of the needs of the export industries, particularly textiles, and the resulting shortage of raw cotton and rayon pulp caused a serious slump in exports. A shrinkage in exchange available for the importation of essential war materials was quickly felt.[29] To solve the problem a "link" system was developed in the summer of 1938. Imports of raw materials were linked with exports of finished products containing them; raw cotton with

[24] New Zealand adopted import licensing in December 1938 for substantially similar reasons. See B. R. Turner, "The State and Industry," *Economic Record* (Melbourne), Vol. XV, October 1939, Supplement, p. 118.
[25] See summary of the Japanese text in *Tokyo Asahi*, August 13, 1937, p. 192, and English translation in Sebald, *op. cit.*, pp. 159-62.
[26] An English translation of the text is given in Sebald, *op. cit.*, pp. 143-58.
[27] *Tokyo Asahi*, August 31, 1938, p. 412.
[28] *Ibid.*, April 7, 1938, p. 84. The Japanese text of the law appears in *ibid.*, September 5, 1937, p. 70. For an English translation see Sebald, *op. cit.*, pp. 129-40.
[29] On current trade problems see M. S. Farley, "The Impact of War on Japan's Foreign Trade," *Far Eastern Survey*, VIII, 11, May 24, 1939, pp. 123-8.

cotton yarn and piece goods, pulp with rayon, bristles with brushes, etc. Each manufacturer was permitted imports on the basis of both his earlier completed exports and his promise to manufacture and export his product within a fixed period of months. Inauguration of the link system was made possible by the establishment of a special revolving exchange fund with 300 million yen of the Bank of Japan specie reserve. While involving some administrative difficulties, the link system seems to have benefited export industries without impairing effective control of exchange.[30]

Licensing of exchange transactions, specific restrictions on commodity imports and exports, and the link system are three stages in Japan's war-time control of her foreign exchange. Like the other measures of promotion and control, each has imposed additional duties on overworked officials of the Department of Finance, the Department of Commerce and Industry, or the Bank of Japan. Each has also required adjustments of interests between the many individuals or corporations engaged in foreign trade and production for export. This adjustment is difficult, arbitrary, and irritating. Desire for its simplification appears to be a dominant factor in the reappearance of the old trend toward monopolies or semi-monopolies under government control.

Semi-official Corporate Monopolies

Monopolies as a means to trade promotion are nothing new to Japan, or to most other countries, but a cursory survey of some recent examples will help to show the reasons leading to their establishment in increasing numbers. They have been particularly noticeable in the shipping and fishing industries, but now seem to be sprouting rapidly in other fields.

Overseas shipping has long been subsidized in Japan. Sub-

[30] See Taniguchi Kichihiko, "The Link System in Japan" and "The Development of the Link System in Japan," *Kyoto University Economic Review*, XIV, 2 and 3, April and July, 1939, respectively. An interesting link by which exportation of a new 10,000 ton vessel to Brazil is to be permitted in return for importation of sufficient raw materials for an equivalent vessel and of 25,000 tons of old bottoms is reported by Prince T. Iwakura in "Senji Keizai ni okeru waga Kaiun Seisaku" (Our Shipping Policy in War Time Economics), *Taiheiyo*, (The Pacific), III, 1, January 1940, p. 71. See also *Trans-Pacific*, October 5, 1939, p. 11. Links between exported Japanese paper and imported Manila hemp and between exported rope and imported hemp and jute were reported in the *Tokyo Asahi*, August 27, 1938, p. 360.

sidy laws, sometimes linked to mail contracts, have been directed to qualitative as well as quantitative progress and have been enacted in consideration of the contribution of a strong merchant marine both to national defense and to a favorable balance of international payments. These acts require no detailed explanation as they are very similar to those applied by other maritime powers. What is more interesting here is that, although it has not yet embarked on state ownership and operation, the government of Japan has been gradually impelled toward means of shipping control more economical and effective than subsidies.

Rationalization of shipping routes was one of the first steps. Originally accomplished by private agreement under official persuasion, it is now legally enforceable under the Navigation Routes Control Law (*Koro Tosei Ho*) passed by the Diet in May 1936 and in force from August 1st of that year. The law provides for a Navigation Routes Control Commission (*Koro Tosei Iinkai*).[31] Mergers of the shipping lines serving specific areas have been found expedient as a means toward more effective competition and negotiation in the trade disputes, for example, with the Dutch East Indies and with Australia.

Since the war, control has, where possible, been exercised through the Autonomous Shipping Control Commission, an organization of the seven leading shipping firms for the adjustment of rates and allocation of bottoms.[32] The government, however, enjoys full legal powers to regulate the acquisition, chartering, disposal and operation of ocean-going vessels under an Emergency Shipping Control Law (*Rinji Sempaku Kanri Ho*).[33] To make this control more effective, particularly over the routes which have been over-taxed because of the demands of the war and of the new development of heavy industry in Japan, two new national policy concerns have recently been formed—the Japan Sea Marine Transportation Company (*Nippon Kai Kaiun Kaisha*) in May and the East Asia Shipping

---

[31] For the appointment of this Commission see *Tokyo Asahi*, August 1, 1936, p. 9.

[32] See *Trans-Pacific*, June 1, 1939, p. 33.

[33] The law is summarized in the *Japan Year Book, 1939-40*, pp. 292-3. For a general discussion of shipping policy see Prince T. Iwakura, "Senji Keizai ni okeru waga Kaiun Seisaku" (Our Shipping Policy in War-Time Economics), *Taiheiyo*, III, 1, January 1940, pp. 68-73.

Company (*Toa Kaiun Kabushiki Kaisha*) in August 1939—monopolizing shipping between Japan and China, respectively.[34]

Fishing and shipping are closely related and have shown similar trends. The Japan-Russia Fishery Company (*Nichi-Ro Gyogyo Kaisha*) is a good example of a state-promoted monopoly. Fishing, an industry probably more vital to Japan than to any other country, had long been under state protection and guidance through subsidy, compulsory inspection of export products, and technical aid. The industry in northern waters was, however, affected by three special problems: the chronic dispute with Russia over coastal fishing rights and the necessity of competing with a Russian state monopoly in the annual auction of fishing lots; restrictions on methods and catches in the interest of conservation; and, related to the latter, the complicated adjustment of interests between those engaged in coastal and pelagic fishing. These problems could be simplified by the amalgamation of all Japanese fishing interests in Russian waters in a single corporation. With this in view the merger in the Nichi-Ro concern of all smaller interests was actively promoted by the Japanese Government until its accomplishment early in 1935.[35] The North Seas Fishery Supervision Law (*Hokuyo Gyogyo Torishimari Ho*), adopted in the spring of 1935, facilitates further developments in this same direction, and a larger merger including the floating crab canneries is not unlikely.[36]

A few more examples from miscellaneous fields will round out the picture of this new trend which seems to be gaining momentum. The Japan Export Hosiery Company (*Dai Nippon Yushutsu Meriyasu Kabushiki Kaisha*) was formed in Osaka in August 1938 by both manufacturers and exporters to monopolize hosiery exports and thereby simplify the operation of the link system.[37] Similar companies for dealing with other goods have been reported.[38] Toward the end of 1938 the Japan-

[34] *Trans-Pacific*, April 27, 1939, p. 18; August 10, 1939, p. 18; April 27, 1939, p. 22. *Oriental Economist*, VI, 9, September 1939, pp. 610-11.

[35] *Tokyo Asahi*, January 19, 1935, p. 244. On the Japan-Russia Company and northern fisheries in general see Yasuo Nagaharu, "The North Ocean Fishery in Japan's Economic Life," *Far Eastern Survey*, VIII, 9, April 26, 1939, pp. 106-8.

[36] See text of the law in *Tokyo Asahi*, February 27, 1935, p. 365, and of the enforcement regulations, *ibid.*, March 19, 1935, p. 274.

[37] *Tokyo Asahi*, August 25, 1938, p. 332.

[38] See, for example, the Japan Export Umbrella Company, reported in *Tokyo Asahi*, September 3, 1938, p. 38. Others are mentioned in Asahi Isoshi, *The Economic Strength of Japan*, Tokyo, 1939, p. 147.

American Lumber Imports Company was organized after promotion by the Department of Commerce and Industry.[39] Among its objectives was the simplification of estimates of Japan's import needs and of the issuance of exchange permits as well as a greater bargaining power vis-à-vis American lumber exporters organized under the Webb-Pomerene Act. In June 1939 the Japan Marine Products Sales Company was established, under the joint supervision of the Department of Agriculture and Forestry and the Department of Commerce and Industry, for the unification of export sales.[40] Such corporations seem to provide convenient and efficient vehicles of control while leaving administration and adjustment of individual interests largely in private hands. It is probable that they will multiply during the next few years.[41]

Japan's desire to increase her trade is shared by all other countries and most of her methods have ample precedent. Yet each attempt at promotion has involved further governmental control. This has been true regardless of whether the immediate aim was economization of means as in shipping, improved bargaining power as with the northern fisheries and the lumber business, maintenance of currency stability as in exchange control, avoidance of ill feeling abroad as in the curtailment of cotton sales, or fulfillment of international agreements as in the allocation of wool purchases from Australia. Nor has it made any appreciable difference whether the foreign country most directly concerned was Nazi Germany, Soviet Russia, mandated Syria, a British dominion, or the United States. In each case a fairly steady trend away from indirect methods like tariffs, subsidies, and exchange stabilization funds toward more direct control through licensing and government orders is observable, and in each case a private monopoly under government supervision, whether guild, cartel, or new corporation, seems to be the most likely result.[42]

[39] Ivan Elchibegoff, "More Blows at America's Transpacific Timber Trade," *Far Eastern Survey,* VIII, 18, August 30, 1939, pp. 215-17.
[40] *Trans-Pacific,* July 6, 1939, p. 31.
[41] A useful discussion of the economic side of Japan's foreign trade since the war is given in Miriam S. Farley, *The Problem of Japanese Trade Expansion in the Post-War Situation.* I.P.R. Inquiry Series, New York, 1940.
[42] The trend toward "national policy" corporations is well described by Ohara Sei in his article "Kokusaku Kaisha wa Hanran Suru" (National Policy Corporations Overflow), *Kaizo,* XXI, 4, April 1939, pp. 93-9. Ohara gives details as to the proportion of stock held by the government in the most important companies.

Such trends cannot be confined to one segment of an integrated economy. Control was bound to spread from foreign to domestic trade by analogy if not by its effect on prices and production, but these internal aspects are more popularly related to demands for recovery and security, to which we now turn.

2. ECONOMIC RECOVERY AND SECURITY

"Stabilization of the national livelihood" (*kokumin seikatsu antei*) is the Japanese slogan equivalent to the current American catchwords "recovery" and "security." The Japanese phrase became popular somewhat earlier because of the absence of prosperity during the twenties which has already been mentioned. Early or late, however, consensus as to the efficacy of specific solutions like devaluation, red-ink bonds (i.e., pump-priming), or promotion of co-operatives has been equally hard to achieve on both sides of the Pacific. Japanese policies for stabilization of the national livelihood may be divided roughly into two parts as they are aimed at industrial recovery or agricultural security.

Industrial Recovery

Rationalization in a narrow sense became a popular slogan in Japan after 1925 under the stimulation of German and American models.[1] Governmental measures were recommended in December 1929 by the Special Committee on Industrial Rationalization of the Council on Commerce and Industry (*Shoko Shingi-kai Sangyo Gorika ni Kansuru Tokubetsu Iinkai*) and again in February 1930 by the newly established Emergency Industrial Council (*Rinji Sangyo Shingi-kai*) under the chairmanship of Premier Hamaguchi. As a result an Emergency Industrial Rationalization Bureau (*Rinji Sangyo Gori Kyoku*) was established in the Department of Commerce and Industry in June of the latter year.[2] This Bureau subsequently formulated plans for the standardization and simplification of parts

---

[1] Compare the movement promoted through the Federated American Engineering Societies after 1920 by the secretary of commerce, Herbert Hoover, and the work in Germany after 1921 of the *Reichskuratorium für Wirtschaftlichkeit*.

[2] It was perhaps a significant indication of a trend when in January 1937 the Emergency Industrial Rationalization Bureau was re-organized as the Industrial Control Bureau (*Sangyo Tosei Kyoku*).

and products, the spread of scientific industrial management, and the improvement and standardization of bookkeeping and auditing methods and commercial correspondence.[3]

Rationalization, interpreted more broadly to include elimination of unnecessary competition and organization of markets and prices, was conceived as an integral part of this program but required further legislative authorization. The large-scale, heavily capitalized branches of Japanese industry were provided for under the Major Industries Control Law (*Juyo Sangyo Tosei Ho*) which went into effect in August 1931 (under the "liberal" Minseito Cabinet and prior to the Manchurian incident). The purpose of the law was to facilitate industrial self-control by making self-governing agreements between producers in important industries legally enforceable and to ensure proper regard for the public interest in such agreements. Analogies can be found in the British Coal Mining Act of 1930, the German *Kartell Gesetz* of 1926, the American National Industrial Recovery Administration and the German *Gesetz über Errichtung von Zwangskartellen*, both of 1933, and the New Zealand Industrial Efficiency Act of 1936. The industries coming under the Major Industries Control Law are determined by departmental ordinances issued after the consultation of a Control Committee (*Tosei Iinkai*) established for that purpose. Industrial agreements under the law may cover limitation of production or operation, division of fields of production or operation, apportionment of orders, prices and factors related thereto, markets, quantities to be marketed, and co-operative marketing. Agreements must be reported to the appropriate minister of state who may order their abrogation or amendment when he deems them injurious to the public interest or in restraint of a fair profit for the industry concerned or another closely related thereto. The law, originally enacted for five years, was renewed with amendments in 1936.[4] Under it such industries as cotton spinning and weaving, silk spinning and weaving, rayon, paper, carbide, flour, sulphuric acid, cement, copper, sugar, and oil pressing have been cartelized and placed under a measure of state supervision.[5]

[3] See Takahashi Kamekichi, *Nippon Keizai Tosei Ron,* pp. 206-9.
[4] See Kishi Shinsuke, "Juyo Sangyo Tosei Ho" (The Major Industries Control Law), in *Horitsugaku Jiten,* Vol. II, p. 1243-6.
[5] See Takahashi Kamekichi, *Nippon Keizai Tosei Ron,* pp. 219-31.

Support for large industrial organizations and family concerns like Mitsui, Sumitomo, Mitsubishi, and Yasuda led to protests from those engaged in the small-scale industries and trades so typical of Japan. Since anti-trust legislation was deemed undesirable from the point of view of industrial efficiency and international competitive ability, small businessmen could be protected only by facilitating their organization into co-operative units able to provide some of the benefits of cartelization. Since guilds had already been created for the promotion of foreign trade, their use for strictly domestic production and trade was a logical next step. A tendency in this direction had already been evident in 1900 in the substitution of the more general Staple Commodities Guilds Law (*Juyo Bussan Dogyo Kumiai Ho*) for the Staple Exports Guilds Law (*Juyo Yushutsu Hin Dogyo Kumiai Ho*) of 1897, and in the enactment in 1925, along with the Export Guilds Law (*Yushutsu Kumiai Ho*), of a Staple Export Commodities Industrial Guilds Law *(Juyo Yushutsu Hin Kogyo Kumiai Ho)*, but the commodities covered by both acts remained the ones important in the export trade. In April 1931, however, the latter act was amended (becoming simply the *Kogyo Kumiai Ho*) so as to be applicable as well to industries producing for the home market such articles as Japanese umbrellas, ice, and tiles.[6] This extension to domestic affairs was not the only innovation of the 1931 amendment. There were five additional changes of importance: (1) The guilds were authorized to accept deposits and to make loans, thus becoming financial organs for small business. (2) They were permitted to make agreements as to restriction of production and as to prices, such agreements, however, to be reported to and to require the approval of the appropriate government office. (3) The appropriate minister was authorized in case of need to order adherence to guild rules by outsiders. (4) The appropriate minister was authorized to issue orders to the guilds both to correct and to prevent abuses. (5) The provisions for provincial and national associations of guilds were strengthened.

These provisions for the organization of small-scale indus-

[6] Melville H. Walker, to whom the author is indebted for many useful suggestions and criticisms, has recently completed a doctoral dissertation at the University of California on "Manufacturers' Guilds in Japanese Small Scale Industries," in which he analyzes the practical results of the Industrial Guilds Law.

tries are very similar to those for heavy industries in the Major Industries Control Law. It is worth noting that these two laws, which form the model and foundation for almost all subsequent industrial control in Japan, were enacted under the leadership of the "liberal" Minseito Cabinet of Hamaguchi, Wakatsuki, and Shidehara well before the Manchurian incident. They were both desired by private business and were drafted as steps toward economic recovery; consideration of any possible relation to national defense was only secondary.

The allegedly "reactionary" Inukai and Saito Cabinets prepared the next step—an almost identical Commercial Guilds Law (*Shogyo Kumiai Ho*), facilitating the organization and control of medium and small-scale commercial undertakings as well as industrial ones. This was promulgated in September 1932. Since that date government support and, incidentally, control of all types of guilds has been increased by subsidies for various joint functions and installations. Attention has been directed particularly to strengthening guild finances to meet the complaint that small-scale businesses find it difficult to secure adequate capital on reasonable terms. The latest step in this direction was the establishment on December 1, 1936, of the Central Depository for Commercial and Industrial Guilds (*Shoko Kumiai Chuo Kinko*). The Depository, authorized by a special statute,[7] enjoys, like such other great semi-public institutions as the Industrial Bank and the Hypothec Bank, special privileges of debenture issue and access to the low-interest funds of the Treasury Deposits Bureau.

The similarity of this guild system to the code-making authority provided in the American National Industrial Recovery Act should not be overlooked. While the Japanese legislation has not always been effective, it has also not been a spectacular failure as was the American N.I.R.A. Its comparative success may be explained at least in part by the constitutional authority of the government to enforce its provisions by something more than verbal blasts against those who disregard the rules and by the greater experience of Japanese businessmen and officials with co-operative trade associations.

Monopolies bring with them price control. Avoidance of artificially high prices detrimental to national livelihood was the primary objective of the provisions for governmental super-

[7] The *Shoko Kumiai Chuo Kinko Ho*, passed by the 69th Diet in May 1936.

vision in both the Major Industries Control Law and the various guild laws. Control over prices was exercised in isolated instances well before 1937, particularly in the steel and oil industries and others under special statutes (not to mention such public utilities as electricity, street-cars, railways, etc., in which rate control is a commonplace in other countries). It was not until the winter of 1936-7, however, that price control on a large scale became an immediate possibility. Finance Minister Yuki expressed concern over rising prices in February, and on April 10, 1937, he told the press that either departmental ordinances or administrative measures to control prices must soon be invoked. In May an Emergency Price Policy Commission (*Rinji Bukka Taisaku Iinkai*) with consumer representation was established.[8] No serious measures were taken until August 3, 1937, after hostilities had begun in China, when an ordinance was promulgated authorizing the government to warn profiteers and fix prices. Emergency war measures caused price rises in every direction and it was many months before the government, aided by a re-organized Price Commission (later headed by ex-Minister of Finance Ikeda Seihin), gradually, and only partially, checked the rapid advance in living and production costs by specific orders for price reductions or fixations, for price tags on all retail goods and, in a few cases, for rationing by card.[9] On the whole, price and consumption control in Japan has been less drastic than it was in most countries during the World War: cotton goods have almost disappeared from the home market and products containing leather or metal have been seriously restricted, but near self-sufficiency has obviated rationing of food supplies.[10] Price control has been hastened and generalized by war conditions but would probably have come in 1937 or 1938 even without the hostilities in China. It is logically related to policies adopted prior to the Manchurian incident.[11]

[8] The statute of the Commission is given in the *Tokyo Asahi*, May 6, 1937, p. 87.

[9] See "Wartime Price Control," *Oriental Economist*, V, 6, June 1938, pp. 357-60, and "Commodity Price Control," *ibid.*, VI, 5, May 1939, pp. 305-7.

[10] Rationing may yet become necessary, however, if too drastic price control, combined with a shortage of labor and fertilizers, should cause a fall in agricultural production as it threatens to do.

[11] On recent attempts to control prices and their shortcomings see Kurt Bloch, "Inflation and Prices in the Yen Bloc," *Far Eastern Survey*, VIII, 16, August 2, 1939, pp. 183-90.

The industrial recovery program in Japan has emphasized rationalization of the organization and operation of industry in order to preserve both profitability and competitive ability in the international market. Public works, direct relief, the armaments boom, and the general policy of cheap money and liberal government spending have also been regarded as parts of the recovery program, but discussion of these aspects will be reserved for other parts of this study.

Agricultural Security

The problems of agriculture easily lead to requests for state aid because of the difficulties of private organization on any large scale and the severe fluctuations in prices due to natural hazards and inflexible demand. In Japan the farm problem is linked with that of the fishing villages, but little real relief for small-scale fishing enterprises has been provided except through state aid to co-operatives, the provision of low-interest capital, establishment of public markets, and encouragement of insurance for fishing boats. Price control is scarcely feasible in view of the perishable nature of the product.

Rice and silk are the two agricultural staples in Japan which have attracted legislation most frequently. They occupy the place in the farm problem held by wheat and cotton in the United States. Producers of both were hard hit about 1930-2 as a result of a heavy mortgage burden acquired in days of higher prices, bad harvests, the decline of world prices, and a terrible slump in silk sales and prices due to competition from rayon and the depression in the United States. After 1931 farm relief or agricultural security became an insistent political demand in Japan, but farm legislation was enacted long before the 1929 depression. This was true not only of technical aid through inspection of eggs and seeds, experimental stations, and scientific advice, but also of more advanced methods of market control.

A market stabilization plan based on the concept of the "Ever Normal Granary" of Wang An-shih (later borrowed by Secretary Wallace) was inaugurated in 1921 under the Rice Law (*Beikoku Ho*). It was amended in 1925 to include price regulation as an objective. Control over rice imports was extended to Taiwan in 1926, to Korea in 1928, and to Karafuto in 1930. In 1933 the Rice Law was replaced by the Rice Control Law (*Beikoku Tosei Ho*) which authorized the government to stabilize prices by setting a minimum price at which it would purchase rice on the open market and a maximum price at which it would sell. A Rice Control Commission (*Beikoku Tosei Iinkai*) was established to advise on the operation of the new measures. The Rice Control Law has been frequently amended but its basic principles have remained unchanged.[12] In the meantime, as a result of objections to the excessive margin between the farmer's receipts for his rice on the one hand and retail prices on the other, the government enacted three measures over the active opposition of rice merchants. The Rice Autonomous Control Law (*Beikoku Jichi Kanri Ho*) of 1936 provided for the semi-compulsory organization of rice dealers in order to secure market control under official supervision. At the same time an act for governmental subsidy to storage facilities for unhulled rice was passed to help farmers escape losses caused by the dumping of crops at low harvest prices (*Momi Kyodo Chozo Josei Ho*). Finally in 1939, under the Rice Distribution Control Law (*Beikoku Haikyu Tosei Ho*), a national-policy "Japan Rice Company" was organized to guide the large-scale rice trade, control the rice futures markets (reduced, incidentally, from 17 to 2), and to monopolize the importation and sale to local dealers of Formosan rice.[13] Prior to 1937 the main problem had been that of assuring a decent return to the farmer, but since the outbreak of hostilities in China the same provisions have been directed toward keeping food prices down while assuring ample supplies both for home consumption and for the army.

The silk problem has had a strikingly similar history.[14] Provision for inspection of silk and of silk-worm egg cards for export was made early in the Meiji era. Further steps to improve the quality and the supply and to encourage the organization of the producers were taken in the Silk Industry Law (*San Shi Gyo Ho*) of 1911. Inspection and grading of all silk for export was made compulsory by the Export Silk Inspection Law

[12] The Law in regard to Temporary Rice Measures (*Beikoku no Okyu Sochi ni Kansuru Horitsu*) of September 10, 1937, merely excepted from the provisions of the Rice Control Law purchases of rice for army or navy use. See *Tokyo Asahi*, September 3, 1937, p. 31.

[13] See "Production and Distribution of Rice," *Tokyo Gazette*, No. 23, May 1939, pp. 1-5; *Trans-Pacific*, May 11, 1939, p. 4; August 10, 1939, p. 19; August 17, 1939, p. 18.

[14] For a good general description of silk legislation through 1934 see Ino Sekiya, "San Shi" (Silk Thread), *Horitsugaku Jiten*, II, pp. 1065-72.

(*Yushutsu Sei Shi Kensa Ho*) of the same year. While silk exports made great progress during the years of the American boom, there were considerable fluctuations in price, and expansion led to other abuses. As a result, the Minseito Cabinet sought to apply to silk in 1929, 1930, and 1931 measures similar to those adopted for rice and for other commodities. The Silk Price Stabilization Credits Guarantee Law (*Shika Antei Yushi Hosho Ho*) of 1929 (in force September 1, 1929) was intended to promote price stability by extending to banks guarantees enabling them to make loans on the security of silk held in storage pending better prices or market conditions. It was doomed to failure by the Wall Street crash of 1929 and the resultant collapse of the silk market in the United States. The banks were left holding large quantities of silk, and both they and the silk producers had to be saved from bankruptcy in 1932 by the Law for Purchase of Silk held as Security for Silk Price Stabilization Loans (*Shika Antei Yushi Tampo Sei Shi Baishu Ho*) and the Law for Remedial Disposition of Losses on Silk Price Stabilization Loans (*Shika Antei Yushi Sonshitsu Zengo Shori Ho*) by which the government shared an increased proportion of the loss and took over the stored stocks, which were depressing the market.[15] An attempt at autonomous control through a national organization of private dealers, the Imperial Silk Company (*Teikoku San Shi Kabushiki Kaisha*), failed for similar reasons.

More lasting improvements were sought through the Silk Industry Guilds Law (*San Shi Gyo Kumiai Ho*) of 1931 (prior to the Manchurian incident) which made legal provision for the organization of local guilds for each branch of silk production or trade, their association in national unions, and an all-inclusive Japan Central Silk Association (*Nippon Chuo San Shi Kai*) to regulate the entire business. The appropriate minister of state was given authority to order the formation of guilds when necessary, and once a guild was organized, membership was made compulsory for all persons in the region engaged in that branch of the industry. In 1932 silk reeling was placed under a license system and the government was authorized to

[15] Disposal of the "canned" silk was limited to new markets or uses. It is only since the war in China that the government has been able to dispose of this stored surplus. See *Trans-Pacific*, May 4, 1939, p. 44. The United States government has also recently expressed the hope of clearing surplus stored commodities in the war boom.

issue orders regarding it under the Silk Reeling Industry Law (*Sei Shi Gyo Ho*). Co-operative organization among small producers and the limitation of new installations were sought. Two years later the Silk Worm Eggs Control Law (*Gen San Shu Kanri Ho*) placed the production and distribution of eggs under strong government control in order to reduce production costs through improved and standardized varieties. The Export Silk Transactions Law (*Yushutsu Sei Shi Torihiki Ho*) of 1934 placed silk exports under governmental license and compelled a public record of all transactions. The appropriate minister was also given added authority to control the silk trade in case of need. The silk guilds were strengthened and the cocoon trade was placed under control in 1936 by the amendment of two earlier statutes and the enactment of the Cocoon Disposal Control Law (*San Ken Shori Tosei Ho*).[16] Finally, the methods of the *Beikoku Tosei Ho* of 1933 were applied to silk in 1937 by the Silk Price Stabilization Arrangements Law (*Shika Antei Shisetsu Ho*) and an associated Special Accounts Law (*Shika Antei Shisetsu Tokubetsu Kaikei Ho*). Under these acts the government, acting with the advice of a Silk Price Stabilization Commission (*Shika Antei Iinkai*), was authorized to purchase and sell silk on the open market at officially determined minimum and maximum prices respectively.[17]

Restrictions on the cotton industry as a result of the hostilities in China since 1937 have led indirectly to increased domestic consumption of silk, a sharp rise in silk prices, and a consequent threat to Japanese silk exports. The problem of control has thus been suddenly changed from price support to price limitation and from production curtailment to promotion. To meet these new conditions Article 8 of the General Mobilization Act may be applied. It is reported that minimum quotas for production and export will be fixed and enforced, that a Central Cocoon Price-Fixing Commission will be authorized to fix prices and that the Imperial Silk Company will be given a monopoly of the export business.[18] This rounds out

[16] See *Tokyo Asahi*, February 27, 1935, p. 374; May 21, 1936, p. 287.
[17] See *Tokyo Asahi*, March 21, 1937, p. 343.
[18] See *Trans-Pacific*, July 6, 1939, p. 33. For a sample of such a state export monopoly in an Anglo-Saxon democracy, compare the New Zealand Primary Products Marketing Act of 1936 and its application to the export trade in dairy products. E.g., H. Belshaw, "Guaranteed Prices in Operation," *The Economic Record* (Melbourne), Vol. XV, October 1939, Supplement, pp. 69-81.

measures taken to date for control of the silk industry. As in the case of rice, the trend has been continuous since before the Manchurian incident and has been motivated primarily by the search for agricultural security.

Aside from this special control of staple commodities, more general aid to farm security has been given through the promotion of co-operatives, regulation of the fertilizer industry, the rural reconstruction movement, and farm credits. Farm co-operatives have a particularly long history. They are known as *kumiai*, like the guilds already mentioned, from which frequently they are legally indistinguishable. They are organized under a bewildering number of statutes and have provincial and national unions to facilitate their functions which include marketing, purchasing, packing and shipping, storage, and financing. They have been actively encouraged by the government through tax exemptions, provision of capital, and expert guidance. In 1936, according to the Department of Agriculture and Forestry, some fifteen thousand societies had over six million members, loans to members exceeded one billion yen, and sales to members amounted to about half a billion yen. Although the co-operatives are not so numerous or so strong as students of Japanese agrarian economics believe desirable, their growth and the governmental aid which they receive have provoked repeated protests from organizations of the small businessmen with whom they compete.[19]

The rural reconstruction movement (*Nosangyoson Keizai Kosei Undo*), which was inaugurated by action of the special rural relief session of the Diet in 1932, is closely related to the co-operatives. With governmental funds for research and guidance, its program starts with education to improve the spirit of community co-operation in rural villages, and proceeds from this to strengthening co-operative purchasing or marketing, joint sponsorship of land readjustment, flood control and irrigation works, and mutual aid in harvesting, child care, etc. This improved community efficiency is supplemented by family education in economy, budgeting, and home industry.[20]

---

[19] See, for example, the resolutions of the National Conference on Protection of Commercial Rights held in Tokyo December 6, 1935. *Tokyo Asahi*, December 7, 1935, p. 96. See also Galen M. Fisher, "The Cooperative Movement in Japan," *Pacific Affairs*, XI, 4, December 1938, pp. 478-91.
[20] See Nasu Shiroshi, "Nosangyoson Keizai Kosei Keikaku" (Farm, Mountain, and Fishing Village Economic Reconstruction Plans), *Keizaigaku Jiten*, Supplement, pp. 450-2.

The supply and the price of fertilizer have been crucial problems in every plan for agricultural security because Japan's efforts to combat land shortage by more intensive cultivation have required wide use of a variety of fertilizers to maintain fertility. Cartelization of the industry both at home and abroad has increased the farmer's problem. State control has long been urged by farm organizations; it was advocated by officials in the Fertilizer Investigation Commission of the Department of Agriculture and Forestry (*Hiryo Chosa Iinkai*) in 1927; a Fertilizer Control Bill (*Hiryo Kanri Ho An*) was put forward by the Tanaka Cabinet in 1929 but failed of passage. The Okada Cabinet sponsored another bill in 1935, but its adoption was delayed until the special session of the Diet in May 1936, following the February 26th incident.[21] The Staple Fertilizers Industry Control Law (*Juyo Hiryo Gyo Tosei Ho*) placed fertilizer production and distribution under a license system, made co-operatives for the various branches compulsory, authorized the co-operatives to control production and price subject to official approval, and empowered the government to regulate importation and to issue necessary orders to the industry which was recognized as affected with the public interest.[22] Under this statute, first enforced in May 1936, prices of ammonium sulphate, calcium cyanamide, and super-phosphates have been controlled, the last since November 1938.[23] Since price control during a war boom might lead to failure of supply or hoarding, the special 72nd Diet passed a Temporary Fertilizer Distribution Control Law (*Rinji Hiryo Haikyu Tosei Ho*) which empowered the government, when necessary, to issue ordinances compelling production and sale of fertilizers and to enforce them by investigation, punishment, and obligatory reports.[24] Finally, a few months later, the 73rd Diet authorized the creation of a Japan Ammonium Sulphate Company (*Nippon Ryuan Kabushiki Kaisha*) under thoroughgoing official control and empowered the government to order persons or corporations engaged in the manufacture of ammonium sulphate to enlarge or improve their equipment, to increase production,

[21] Takahashi Kamekichi, *Nippon Keizai Tosei Ron*, pp. 396-8.
[22] Kishi Shinsuke, "Tosei Sangyo Rippo" (Economic Control Legislation), *Horitsugaku Jiten*, Vol. III, p. 2025.
[23] *Trans-Pacific*, September 8, 1938, p. 19.
[24] See text of the statute in *Tokyo Asahi*, September 4, 1937, p. 54. English translation in Sebald, *op. cit.*, pp. 171-2.

or to dispose of their product to the new corporation. In return, such persons were given special tax exemptions, financial privileges, and guarantees against loss (*Ryusan Ammonia Zosan oyobi Haikyu Tosei Ho*).[25]

Unadjusted farm debts constituted a serious threat to Japanese banks as well as to Japanese agriculture in 1932. Their reduction was one objective of the rural reconstruction movement already mentioned. Provision for adjustment by arbitration, compulsory if necessary, was made in the Monetary Debts Conciliation Law (*Kinsen Saimu Rinji Chotei Ho*) of 1932. This act was originally applicable only to debts of one thousand yen or less contracted before its promulgation, and its validity was limited to three years, but it was renewed in amended and semi-permanent form in 1934.[26]

Farmers' co-operatives for the purposes of mutual aid in debt liquidation and the joint guarantee of loans were authorized and given government aid through the Farm Village Debt Adjustment Law (*Noson Fusai Seiri Ho*) and the Farm Household Debt Adjustment Co-operatives Law (*Noka Fusai Seiri Kumiai Ho*) of 1933.[27] At about the same time, by means of the Law for Credits on Immovables and for Indemnification for Losses (*Fudosan Yushi oyobi Sonshitsu Hosho Ho*) of 1932,[28] and by provision for loans on livestock, farm machinery, and small fishing boats through rural credit co-operatives, fishing co-operatives, and other corporations determined by ordinance (under the Agricultural Chattel Credit Law—*Nogyo Dosan*

[25] Text in *Tokyo Asahi*, March 13, 1938, p. 184. On recent difficulties in the enforcement of these various statutes see M. S. Farley, "Japan's Fertilizer Problem Still Unsolved," *Far Eastern Survey*, VIII, 6, March 15, 1939, pp. 73-4.

[26] Conciliation was a well-known procedure in Japan even before it was legally authorized or required in such statutes as the Rented Lands and Houses Conciliation Law (*Shakuchi Shakuya Chotei Ho*) of 1922, the Farm Tenancy Conciliation Law (*Kosaku Chotei Ho*) of 1924, and the Commercial Matters Conciliation Law (*Shoji Chotei Ho*) and Labor Disputes Conciliation Law (*Rodo Sogi Chotei Ho*) of 1926. Ikeda Torajiro, "Chotei" (Arbitration), *Horitsugaku Jiten*, Vol. III, pp. 1907-17. On the Farm Tenancy Conciliation Law see "A New Method of Tenancy Disputes in Japan," *International Labor Review*, March 1925, pp. 381-8. A Domestic Disputes Conciliation Law was promulgated on March 16, 1939 (*Jinji Chotei Ho*). See "A System for Arbitration of Domestic Disputes," *Tokyo Gazette*, No. 23, May 1939, pp. 10-19.

[27] Otsuki Masao, "Noka no Fusai" (Farm Household Debts), *Keizaigaku Jiten*, Supplement, pp. 444-5.

[28] Iwasaki Hiroshi, "Jikyoku Kyokyu Kinyu Taisaku" (Credit Policy for Solution of the Crisis), *ibid.*, Supplement, pp. 222-3.

Shinyo Ho—of 1933[29]), the government sought to augment the supply of capital in rural areas by authorizing the *Kogyo Ginko*, the *Noko Ginko*, and other semi-public financial institutions to purchase the farm mortgages then choking the private banks.

The Central Bank of the Production Co-operatives (*Sangyo Kumiai Chuo Kinko*) was also strengthened and insured against losses on farm loans. These various acts did not solve the farm crisis although they undoubtedly provided at least temporary relief. Their objectives were much the same as those of recent farm legislation in America—relief of both farmers and bankers through the refinancing of farm debts and aid to independent small farmers and tenants. Since the war in China several new steps have been taken in this direction. The Temporary Farm Debts Settlement Law (*Rinji Noson Fusai Shori Ho*) of 1938 provided for the adjustment of debts contracted by families of persons killed or injured while on service in China.[30] The Farm Lands Adjustment Law (*Nochi Chosei Ho*, 1938) gave local committees extensive powers for the adjustment of tenancy disputes, the communal cultivation of the lands of persons on active service, and the acquisition of lands for co-operative cultivation.[31] Finally, the Agricultural Insurance Law[32] (*Nogyo Hoken Ho*) and Agricultural Re-insurance Special Accounts Law (*Nogyo Saihoken Tokubetsu Kaikei Ho*) of 1938 have provided limited national assistance to co-operative organizations for crop insurance. Prior to 1937 there was a certain undercurrent of disagreement as to the relative urgency of farm relief, arms expansion, and economy, but this disagreement seldom came to the surface to any marked extent. The government has, on the whole, been slow to grant extensive direct monetary subsidies to farming but has been somewhat ahead of the two major parties in the Diet in advocating other legislative assistance to tenants, rural debtors, and small independent farmers.[33]

[29] Kusumi Issei, "Dosan Teito" (Chattel Mortgages), *ibid.*, Supplement, pp. 380-1.

[30] See explanation in the *Tokyo Gazette*, No. 13, July 1938, p. 53.

[31] See Department of Agriculture and Forestry, "On the Law for Agrarian Adjustment," *Tokyo Gazette*, Nos. 9 and 10, March-April 1938, pp. 5-9. The text of the Act with amendments appears in the *Tokyo Asahi*, January 24, 1938, p. 317; March 4, 1938, p. 52; and March 9, 1938, p. 124.

[32] Text in *Tokyo Asahi*, March 5, 1938, p. 67.

[33] A general description of Japanese agrarian policy is contained in Nasu Shiroshi, "Ziele und Ausrichtung der japanischen Agrarpolitik in der Gegenwart," *Weltwirtschaftliches Archiv*, XLVI, 1, July 1937, pp. 157-82.

The labor and agrarian parties in the Diet like the *Shakai Taishu-to* and the *Toho-kai* have generally supported government legislation against the opposition of the larger and older parties but have at the same time stigmatized each new act as inadequate.

The government, however, found each step toward recovery and rehabilitation, rural or urban, complicated not only by financial difficulties and disagreement between various sections of the public as to methods and principles, but also by the increasing need of including in all economic plans consideration of the position of Japan's colonies, of Manchukuo, and, more recently, of the occupied areas of China.

3. OVERSEAS DEVELOPMENT AND DOMESTIC CONTROL

Paternalism is particularly current in colonial areas for good as well as bad reasons. Rapid economic development is usually desired, while capital and business ability are scarce and risks high; protection of native populations against exploitation by the highly developed capitalistic industrial and commercial organizations of the homeland is usually a genuine aim of at least a few members of the government. Japan had had little experience in colonial government when she entered the modern scene, but there was nothing to prevent her from following Western advice. One foreign adviser, General Capron, former chief of the United States Bureau of Agriculture, was in part responsible for the early policies of the *Hokkaido Kaitakushi* (Hokkaido Development Administration) which included the establishment by the government of flour mills, beet sugar refineries, breweries, and canneries.[1] When Formosa was annexed following the Sino-Japanese War, sugar production there was developed under special governmental aid and guidance while the salt and camphor industries were expanded as state monopolies. The Government General of Korea early operated coal mines, salt fields, and lumber mills while in recent years, notably under General Ugaki, a measure of economic planning, intended particularly to increase the production of wool, gold, and cotton, has been instituted. Manchuria since the Japanese occupation is the most conspicuous example of all. Its economic development under a sort of state socialism for the benefit of

[1] See Sato Shosuke, "Hokkaido and its Progress in Fifty Years," *Fifty Years of New Japan*. London, 1910, Vol. II, p. 518.

its Chinese inhabitants and the Japanese people rather than for the private gain of Japanese capitalists was advocated by many Japanese army officers. This demand, which was also independently expressed by the *Shakai Minshu-to*, or Social Democratic Party,[2] and by the liberal *Tokyo Asahi* newspaper,[3] met with widespread public approval. Thoroughgoing control of all major industries has become a basic policy of the government of Manchukuo.

Such policies develop more slowly at home, where social contacts and the parliamentary system give private business interests greater influence with the civil service. The time is rapidly passing, however, when domestic and overseas policies can be isolated to any considerable degree. Even before the recent rapid increase in economic control, there was a steady exchange of administrative personnel between the overseas areas and Japan proper, while colonial officials brought back to Japan their belief in and experience with certain methods of administration. Goto Shimpei, for example, returned from a period of service as civil vice-governor of Taiwan convinced that "a monopoly, when judiciously administered, is far more beneficial to the public than any other system."[4] He was subsequently influential in home politics and at one time mayor of Tokyo. The success of the South Manchuria Railway Company and of the Oriental Development Company in Manchuria and Korea has undoubtedly encouraged the establishment of other quasi-state corporations both in Japan proper and overseas. The *Hsing Chung Kung Ssu*, or China Development Company, of 1935 and the North and Central China companies (*Hoku-Shi Kaihatsu Kaisha* and *Chu-Shi Shinko Kaisha*) of November 1938 are only the most recent of many examples.[5]

The economic measures of recent years have brought with them a still greater interchange of influences. Self-sufficiency could not even be considered without the overseas areas. Sugar from Formosa, cotton from Taiwan, Manchuria and China, wool from Hokkaido, Korea and Mongolia, phosphates from

---

[2] The *Shakai Minshu-to* slogan in the February 1932 election was "Put the Rights and Interests in Manchuria in the Hands of the People!" *Tokyo Asahi*, January 23, 1932, 23-11.

[3] See the editorial, *ibid.*, January 6, 1932, 6-7.

[4] Goto Shimpei, "The Administration of Formosa," *Fifty Years of New Japan*, Vol. II, p. 546.

[5] For the latter two see *Trans-Pacific*, November 10, 1938, p. 19.

the Mandated Islands, oil from Karafuto and from Manchurian shale, coal from Fushun, and iron from Anshan were all necessary for the new plans. Control of rice supply and price brought with it complicated problems of adjustment between Japanese, Formosan, and Korean producers. Labor legislation and unemployment relief involved the question of competition from Koreans and Chinese. The overseas areas could not be isolated from Japan, and yet exchange, import, and price control would not work if applied to only a part of the economic unit: they had to be applied to all or to none.

It was the Manchurian occupation which brought the problem to a head. Development of Manchuria in a single economic unit with Japan meant competition with Japanese labor and industry. Japanese were not lacking who viewed the prospect much as American beet-sugar producers view American retention of the Philippines. Japan, however, lacked the abundance of resources which makes American relinquishment of the Philippines relatively easy. While holding Manchuria might be costly and dangerous, it was feared that its renunciation would mean not only loss of face but also acceptance of a permanent second-rate position politically and economically among world powers. That is to say, Manchuria seemed of tremendous economic and strategic importance in any general program of national defense. So Japan remained. Manchuria could not be held without rapid, expensive economic development, but nonrecognition by the United States and the League of Nations checked any possible large-scale influx of foreign capital. Development without such participation was possible only with considerable strain and required the rational and integrated husbanding of the financial and material resources of both Manchuria and Japan.

While the principle of a Japan-Manchukuo economic bloc was thus inherent in Japanese protection of Manchuria, it was only gradually accepted in Japanese business circles as the occupation proved effective and as the various conflicts of interest and personality between different groups were adjusted by gradual compromise. In 1933, for example, employees of the South Manchuria Railway Company demonstrated in protest against the reported desire of the Kwantung Army to extend its control over the railway. The Overseas Department was also dissatisfied because it had not been consulted. No break developed; instead the Army and the Railway found co-operation mutually advantageous. Two years later subordination of the governor of the Kwantung Leased Territory to the commander of the Kwantung garrison led to a strike of protest among the civilian police and administrative officers of the peninsula, but intelligent exercise of his new powers by General Minami soon ironed out the difficulties. For several years there was friction between the army and the Department of Overseas Affairs over the question of the control of Manchurian policies. Abolition of the Overseas Department was repeatedly advocated. Instead the Manchurian Affairs Bureau was created to supervise Japan's new dependency, and the Department of Overseas Affairs survived to co-operate with the new organ. Distrust between the Kwantung Army and Japanese business leaders has been similarly lessened, the young officers gradually softening their attacks on business and the capitalists becoming reconciled to an increasing measure of state control. As the obstacles have been cleared away, co-operation in economic matters between Japan and Manchukuo has become increasingly close. Since a separate volume would be necessary to trace this evolution in any detail, only a few high points can be noted here to indicate the trend.

Autumn 1932. Vice-ministers of the various departments of state met to discuss methods and organization of economic co-operation between Japan and Manchukuo.

March 1933. The Hsinking government announced its intention to entrust the management of all state railways to the South Manchuria Railway. This resulted in the unification of railroad management under a measure of Japanese control exercised through the Kwantung Bureau of the Japanese Embassy in Hsinking.

July 1935. An agreement for the establishment of the Japan-Manchukuo Economic Commission was signed in Hsinking.

August 1935. Matsuoka was appointed president of the South Manchuria Railway to facilitate co-operation between the Railway, the Kwantung Army, and Japanese financial circles.

November 1935. Japan and Manchukuo signed an agreement for the stabilization of the currency of Manchukuo.

November 1935. Manchukuo announced enforcement in December of its new Foreign Currency Exchange Control Law.

Subsequent changes in this control have been co-ordinated with those in Japan.

December 1935. The Bank of Chosen and the Central Bank of Manchu signed an agreement for business co-operation.

May 1936. The Bank of Japan adjusted its purchase price for mined gold to that of Manchukuo in order to check smuggling. Subsequent changes in price have been co-ordinated.

May 1936. The Central Bank of Manchu adjusted its interest rates to the cheap-money policy in Japan.

June 1936. Manchukuo drafted a new industrial control law defining lines of industrial co-operation between Japan and Manchukuo.

June 1936. A treaty between Japan and Manchukuo for the protection of industrial rights was signed.

July-August 1936. Manchukuo co-operated with Japan in retaliation against the Australian tariff.

October 1936. Management of the South Manchuria Railway, the Manchukuo State Railways, and the North Korea Railways was centralized in the Railway General Directorate, Hsinking.

November 1936. The fundamentals of the Manchukuo Five-Year Plan were agreed upon at Hsinking in a joint conference of representatives of Manchukuo, the Kwantung Army, the Japanese Embassy, the Kwantung Bureau, and the South Manchuria Railway.[6]

December 1936. The trade agreement between Germany and Manchukuo in reality constituted a triangular agreement between Japan, Manchukuo, and Germany.

January 1937. The Bank of Chosen turned over its branches in Manchuria to the new Industrial Bank of Manchukuo.

April 1937. Manchukuo licensed exchange for imports in co-operation with the new Japanese trade regulations.

May 1937. The gold reserve of the Bank of Manchu was transferred to the Bank of Japan.

October 1937. The acting vice-chairman of the Manchurian Affairs Bureau (Tokyo) was appointed vice-chairman of the reorganized Planning Board (Tokyo) in order to facilitate integration of domestic and Manchurian affairs.

December 1937. Establishment of the Nippon Industrial Company in Hsinking as the Manchuria Heavy Industrial Development Company (*Manshu Jukogyo Kaihatsu Kaisha*) repre-

[6] *Manchuria Daily News*, November 14, 1936, 1:4.

sented a new stage in the development of the economic policies of Manchukuo and relations with Japanese capital. Increased privileges were granted to private capital, but the company was placed under official supervision.[7]

December 1937. Japan surrendered her extraterritorial rights in Manchukuo and jurisdiction over the South Manchuria Railway zone.

March 1938. Manchukuo co-operated with Japan in checking profiteering in cotton goods.

April 1938. Manchukuo promulgated its Iron and Steel Control Law (*Tekko Tosei Ho*) authorizing control of distribution, thus facilitating co-operation with the Japanese control measures adopted about the same time.[8]

April 1938. General Mobilization Acts were promulgated almost simultaneously in Japan and Manchukuo.

May 1938. Manchukuo announced the revised Five-Year Plan after long consultations between Tokyo and Hsinking. According to Hoshino Naoki, director of the General Affairs Board (Hsinking), the revision was "for the sole purpose of ensuring the smooth development of Japan-Manchukuo 'bloc economy' against the new situation brought about by the China Incident."[9]

July 1938. Exchange control for Manchukuo and for the Kwantung Leased Territory was united in a single office in the Central Bank of Manchu, Hsinking.[10]

August 1938. A special conference on the regulation of agricultural relations among Japan, her colonies, Manchukuo, and China was held in Tokyo.[11]

September 1938. Manchukuo promulgated an Emergency Capital Control Law (*Rinji Shikin Tosei Ho*) closely paralleling that in force in Japan. Under this and the earlier Corporate Debenture Mortgage Trusteeship Law (*Shasai Tampo Ken*

---

[7] The corporate articles of association and the Manchukuo statute for the supervision of the company are given in the *Japan-Manchoukuo Year Book, 1939*, pp. 905-11. The significance of this development is discussed by Yasuo Nagaharu in "Manchukuo's New Economic Policy," *Pacific Affairs*, XI, 3, September, 1938, pp. 323-37.

[8] See summaries in the *Tokyo Asahi*, April 1, 1938, p. 10, and in the *Japan-Manchoukuo Year Book, 1939*, pp. 805-6.

[9] *Manchuria Daily News*, March 15, 1938, 2:1; March 17, 1938, 1:1, 8:4. *Japan-Manchoukuo Year Book, 1939*, pp. 899-901.

[10] *Tokyo Asahi*, Aug. 1, 1938, p. 6.

[11] For the agenda see *Tokyo Asahi*, July 13, 1938, p. 200.

Shintaku Ho), of August 25, 1938, the flow of capital in Manchukuo was canalized and brought under state control. This control has been integrated with that in Japan since 1938.[12]

November 1938. A Japan-Manchukuo-China Economic Council including businessmen from Japan, Manchukuo, Inner Mongolia, and China met in Tokyo.

February 1939. Military officers from Japan, Korea, Manchukuo, and China discussed with government officials in Tokyo the problem of unified mobilization of munitions.

March 1939. Co-ordination between Manchukuo and the Kwantung Leased Territory was provided for on the promulgation by the former of the Cotton Goods Control Law (*Menseihin Tosei Ho*).[13]

April 1939. The Manchukuo post-office network began to handle postal savings transfers and telegraphic exchange transfers for Japan as a convenience for Japanese residents in Manchuria and as an encouragement to the war-savings program.[14]

August 1939. The transfer of many small and medium-sized engineering plants from the Osaka area to Manchukuo was decided upon by the Japanese Government.[15]

These and many other similar events indicate an irregular yet unbroken trend toward the integration of industry in Manchukuo with that in Japan, an integration made possible only by far-reaching control measures on each side.[16] This tendency is still more evident between Japan and her colonies—Formosa, Korea, Karafuto, and the Mandated Islands. Faced with a similar dilemma, the United States has hitherto preferred relinquishing the Philippines to accepting the economic inconveniences and responsibilities involved in integrating them with her own economy. Japan has chosen the other al-

[12] *Tokyo Asahi*, August 16, 1938, p. 210; August 23, 1938, p. 302; September 9, 1938, p. 120; September 21, 1938, p. 280; September 30, 1938, p. 402; January 10, 1939, p. 108. For a general discussion of the integration of control of capital see Inaba Shiro, "Nichi-Man Shikin Tosei no Senji-teki Hoko" (Wartime Trends in Japan-Manchukuo Capital Control), *Mantetsu Chosa Geppo* (South Manchuria Railway Research Monthly), XIX, 4, April 1939, pp. 1-33.

[13] *Tokyo Asahi*, March 25, 1939, p. 332.

[14] *Ibid.*, March 29, 1939, p. 390.

[15] *Trans-Pacific*, August 10, 1939, p. 21.

[16] Some of the difficulties and shortcomings of such measures are discussed by Kurt Bloch in various articles in the *Far Eastern Survey*. E.g., "Coal and Power Shortage in Japan," IX, 4, February 14, 1940, pp. 39-45, and "Yen-Bloc Food Supplies Under Strain," VIII, 21, October 25, 1939, pp. 250-1.

ternative and is now, for better or worse, committed to a policy of assimilation among the colonies, Manchukuo, and Japan proper. Economically this will probably be more advantageous to the colonies than to the homeland because Japan has already embarked on a course of industrial development where the resources are located rather than on one of exploitation of the overseas areas merely as sources of raw materials for industries in Japan proper. Politically, on the other hand, if the program is successful, it means that there can be independence for neither Manchukuo nor Japan, for each new step must mean closer administrative co-operation. The decision has been influenced decisively, although not exclusively, by requirements of national defense which, because of their additional importance for Japan's internal development, are treated in a separate chapter below.

4. NATIONAL DEFENSE

The World War did not cause such drastic economic control in Japan as it did in the United States, Great Britain, France and Germany. Such statutes as the Naval Supplies Ordinance (*Kaigun Kyuyo Rei*) of 1904 were in existence, but it was not until 1918 that a modern law for the mobilization of the munitions industry in a broad sense was enacted. The Munitions Industries Mobilization Law (*Gunju Kogyo Doin Ho*) of that year defined military supplies broadly and authorized supervision, use, or expropriation of the industries producing them.[1] Many of its provisions were never enforced.

Japan could congratulate herself on avoiding some of the inconveniences of war, but her military and naval officers would have served the country poorly indeed had they failed to recognize the greatly enlarged rôle of economic mobilization in the European conflict and to develop new plans of national defense in accordance therewith. This new work of the military and naval general staffs was led by some of the younger officers, like Nagata Tetsuzan, who had served as *attachés* in Europe during the War. Their ideas materialized in 1927 in the establishment of a Resources Bureau (*Shigen Kyoku*) which was to investigate broad problems of national defense and to recommend policies for their solution. The early work of the Bureau led to the promulgation in 1929 of the Resources Investigation

---

[1] See Yanase Ryokan, "Gunju Kogyo Doin" (Mobilization of Military Supplies Industries), *Horitsugaku Jiten*, Vol. I, p. 547.

Law (*Shigen Chosa Ho*) which authorized it to require reports from all branches of industry, and to send out its own investigators when necessary. These reports and investigations have in practice been handled by various regular departments of the government.[2] The Resources Bureau continued its work with little publicity but with a steady flow of new legislation on industries of special military significance to mark its progress. A brief survey of the consequences for a few of these industries will prove illuminating.

Iron and Steel

Production of steel and its products had been a serious concern of the Japanese Government since well before the Meiji Restoration, and the industry was long dominated by the publicly owned Yawata Iron Works. Private concerns were large in scale and small in numbers. Their cartelization was promoted under the Major Industries Control Law of 1931. In addition, of course, indirect control was possible through shipping subsidies, the purchasing policies of the government railways, the army and the navy, and by tariffs and other import restrictions. A law providing for the merger of major iron and steel manufacturing concerns into a single semi-public corporation was passed by the Diet in March 1933 and went into effect shortly afterward. The Japan Iron Manufacturing Company accounts for almost the entire national output of pig iron and for about half the output of steel ingots and steel products.[3]

Early in 1938 an Iron and Steel Control Council (*Tekko Tosei Kyogi-kai*) was established in the Department of Commerce and Industry to set all-inclusive quotas for the importation, production, distribution, and exportation of iron, steel, and their products. Quotas for particular producers are fixed by the Nippon Steel Materials Federation (*Nippon Kozai Rengo-kai*), and those for consumers by various organizations for engineering, mining, electric power, machinery, etc. Quotas are enforceable under the Iron and Steel Distribution Control Regulations (*Tekko Haikyu Tosei Kisoku*), put into effect in

[2] See Tanaka Jiro, "Shigen Chosa" (Resources Investigation), *ibid.*, Vol. II, p. 1087. Compare the strategic minerals investigations of the United States Bureau of Mines under Act of Congress of June 7, 1939.

[3] Compare the New Zealand Iron and Steel Industry Act of 1937, authorizing establishment of a state iron and steel industry with sole rights to mine iron ore in New Zealand. B. Turner, "The State and Industry," *The Economic Record* (Melbourne), Vol. XV, Supplement, October 1939, p. 117.

July 1938.[4] The Nippon Steel Materials Federation also controls the sale of steel products, while pig iron is similarly managed by the Japan-Manchukuo Iron and Steel Sales Company, which represents the Japan Iron Manufacturing Company and the Showa Iron Works (of Manchuria). Early in 1939 scrap iron distribution was added to this imposing organization which is paralleled, of course, by systems of control for non-ferrous metals.[5]

Automobiles

Subsidies to producers of motor vehicles for military use were inaugurated in 1919 under a law passed by the Diet in the previous year (*Gunyo Jidosha Hojo Ho*). Scheduled bus and truck transportation was placed under the control of the Department of Railways by the Motor Vehicles Communications Industry Law (*Jidosha Kotsu Jigyo Ho*) of 1931.[6] Cartelization was made possible by the Major Industries Control Law of 1931, but the Department of Commerce and Industry sought a definite merger of the principal Japanese producers which resulted in the organization of the Motor Car Industrial Company (*Jidosha Kogyo Kabushiki Kaisha*) early in 1933. While this company is privately owned, its progress and control have been facilitated by governmental aid through direct subsidies or the preferential purchase of its products by such public organs as the Department of Railways. Further control, including quotas for the various producers, was made possible by the Automobile Manufacture Industry Law of 1936, and since the outbreak of hostilities in China the increase of motor vehicle production has been an important item in the various three- and five-year plans outlined for Manchukuo and Japan. A special feature of official policy has been the encouragement of the production of vehicles powered by engines burning crude oil, charcoal, or wood, to facilitate economy in imported fuels.

Oil

Within her own territory Japan has only extremely limited

[4] Summary in *Tokyo Asahi*, June 19, 1938, p. 280.
[5] See "War and Steel Industry," *Oriental Economist*, VI, 1, January 1939, pp. 22-4; see also "Copper and Coal Control," *ibid.*, VI, 2, February 1939, pp. 95-8.
[6] Kiyasu Kenjiro, "Jidosha Kotsu Jigyo Ho," *Horitsugaku Jiten*, Vol. II, p. 1152.

oil resources to meet the needs of her civilian population as well as those of her fleet and army. Great Britain, in spite of her political or corporate control of a large fraction of the world's oil supply found it desirable to introduce rationing of gasoline for civilian use in September 1939, less than one month after her declaration of war on Germany. Steps to meet Japan's much more severe problem were naturally taken under consideration at an early date. Measures were proposed by the Fuels Investigation Commission (*Nenryo Chosa Iinkai*) in 1926, by the Council on Commerce and Industry (*Shoko Shingi-k*ai) in 1929, and by a conference of experts from various governmental departments in 1933. A Petroleum Industry Law was finally passed in 1934, giving the government authority to license the business of refining or importing petroleum and its products, to require importers to store at least a six months' supply in Japan at all times, to order reports on business and conduct investigations, and to order price changes, improvements, or expansion of plants, and other steps necessary for the assurance of supply. On the application of these provisions the government was required to consult a newly established Petroleum Industry Commission (*Sekiyugyo Iinkai*). Prices and production and import quotas have since been established by the Department of Commerce and Industry, although application of some of the provisions of the Law was delayed by the long controversy with the American and British oil companies which dominate the import market. Rationing of gasoline used in private vehicles did not go into effect until May 1, 1938, nearly ten months after the Lukouchiao incident, but since then it has become drastic. The mixture of alcohol with gasoline for private consumption became compulsory only after July 1, 1938, but preparation for this step had been made by the establishment of an official alcohol monopoly under legislation passed in March 1937 by the 70th Session of the Diet (*Arukoru Sembai Ho*). Increased production of oil has been promoted not only through official sponsorship of oil-shale distillation at Anshan in Manchuria, but also more generally under the Artificial Oil Manufacture Undertakings Law (*Jinzo Sekiyu Seizo Jigyo Ho*) of 1937, the Imperial Fuel Industry Company, authorized by a statute (*Teikoku Nenryo Kogyo Kabushiki Kaisha Ho*) of the same year, and the Petroleum Resources Development Law (*Sekiyu Shigen Kaihatsu Ho*) of 1938.[7]

Airplanes

Japan has been slow in developing the manufacture of airplanes and civil air transportation. Both had to wait many years for the boom which the aviation industries in Western countries enjoyed during the World War. Since 1932, however, the Army, Navy, Communications, and Railways Departments have vied with each other in promoting aviation through subsidizing manufacture, transportation schedules, and research. Promotion and control of the manufacturing industry were provided by statute in March 1938 (*Kokuki Seizo Jigyo Ho*), and in May 1939 major air transportation companies were merged in the Japan Aviation Company, a national-policy concern (*Dai Nippon Koku Kabushiki Kaisha Ho*).[8]

Electric Power

Army officers were active in the campaign which finally led to governmental control of the electric power and transmission industry in Japan, yet the reasons for control were only in part military; army interest in the matter came only after government control had long been advocated by civil officials. Because of the scarcity of fuels and the abundance of water power, generation and consumption of electricity have developed rapidly in Japan. Prior to 1939 the industry was in the hands of four or five large companies, dominated in turn by Japan's great family trusts. Electric power is the key to the survival of small-scale factories which cannot afford their own power plants; electric power is also the key to the decentralization of industry which is advocated as a solution to the farm problem. Each of these facts has helped to make control of the power industry a symbol of social reform, of the supremacy of national interests over private monopolies. Army leaders favor social reforms as a necessary prerequisite for solidarity behind the lines in time of war; they also favor decentralization of industry because it would help to reduce Japan's excessive vulner-

[7] On recent developments and plans see John R. Stewart, "Japan Still Seeks Oil from Coal and Shale," *Far Eastern Survey*, VIII, 2, January 19, 1939, pp. 22-3.

[8] For a summary of recent developments see Lawrence H. Odell, "Efforts to Stimulate Domestic Airplane Output in Japan," *Far Eastern Survey*, IX, 3, January 31, 1940, pp. 37-8.

ability to air raids. Moreover, electric power is important in the production of light metals—magnesium and aluminum—and of chemicals directly or indirectly related to the armaments industry; and Japan's army leaders were concerned about a possible power shortage in time of war. It is not surprising then that control of the power industry should have been advocated by both the army and the Social Mass Party, the most socialistic party in the Diet, as well as by many civil officials connected with neither the army nor the navy. Although talked of much earlier, such control first became a major item in the platform of Premier Hirota's cabinet in 1936. Control was opposed by many Diet members and by the private power industry. The army kept its promise to leave application of such economic programs to the civilian departments, and the cabinet preferred negotiation to dictatorship. As a result, progress was slow. It was not until March 1938 that the Diet passed, with amendments, the Electric Power Control Law (*Denryoku Kanri Ho*), the Japan Electric Power Generation and Transmission Company Law (*Nippon Hasso Den Kabushiki Kaisha Ho*) and associated statutes. The company, not formally inaugurated until April 1, 1939, is the new agency of government control in which are merged the interests and facilities of the major generating and distributing systems.[9]

We have not exhausted the list of industries which have been promoted or controlled on the advice of the Resources Bureau because of their relation to national defense. A more complete tabulation would include the fertilizer and shipping industries which have been discussed elsewhere. In fact, almost any control measure may be interpreted as a contribution to national defense to the degree that it is calculated to increase economic strength and general welfare. There are also a few more cases, like encouragement of horse breeding or of production of non-ferrous metals, where the connection is quite direct; but we have given enough examples to show the trend.

The extensive application of special statutes prior to July 1937 simplified the problem of meeting the emergency needs caused by the hostilities in China and helps to explain why Japan has been so leisurely in the adoption and application of

[9] "Power Monopoly Concern Starts Business," *Oriental Economist*, VI, 5, May 1939, pp. 325-6. "The National Electric Power Policy in Operation," *Tokyo Gazette*, No. 24, June, 1939, pp. 15-16.

her General Mobilization Act (compared to the promulgation of the new Emergency Powers Bill in Great Britain on August 24, 1939, before the actual commencement of hostilities with Germany). The special 72nd Diet, meeting at the beginning of September 1937, had to pass a statute applying the out-of-date Munitions Industries Mobilization Law (*Gunju Kogyo Doin Ho*) of 1918 only because that statute was limited by its original terminology to a state of "war."[10] Aside from this adjustment in wording and special war appropriations, the most important products of the special session were the Emergency Capital Adjustment Law (*Rinji Shikin Chosei Ho*) and the Emergency Shipping Control Law (*Rinji Sempaku Kanri Ho*).

The General Mobilization Law (*Kokka Sodoin Ho*) was enacted by the regular 73rd Diet in March 1938 after long and heated debate in both the House of Representatives and the House of Peers.[11] It is a general enabling statute in broad terms not very different in content from the emergency legislation adopted in both France and Great Britain recently with little or no discussion in the Chamber of Deputies or in Parliament.[12] Its numerous articles permit, but do not of themselves institute, a wide variety of controls. Many of these powers had not been utilized after two years of war. Application is effected by means of Imperial ordinances. The government thereby receives a liberal accession of power since such ordinances do not require the assent of the Diet. The cabinet is not completely free, however, for drafts of ordinances must be sub-

[10] This statute was replaced by the General Mobilization Law on the promulgation of the latter. The texts of the 1937 amendment and of the major provisions of the 1918 statute are translated in Sebald, *op. cit.*, pp. 173-4.

[11] Promulgated April 1, 1938. A translation of the text of the law is given in *Trans-Pacific*, Feb. 24, 1938, pp. 16-17. See also Kathleen Barnes, "Japanese Government Given Blank Check," *Far Eastern Survey*, VII, 7, April 6, 1938, pp. 79-81; Miriam S. Farley, "The National Mobilization Controversy in Japan," *ibid.*, VII, 3, February 1, 1939, pp. 25-30.

[12] Compare also the war-time emergency powers of the president of the United States and their exercise, for example, through the War Industries Board. Proposals for an industrial mobilization act giving the president authority to fix prices, control profits, and conscript the resources and directing personnel of industry have been before the American Congress almost continuously since 1922, were recommended by the War Policies Commission under President Hoover in 1932, and were hotly debated in the spring of 1938. While not yet on the statute books, such measures would undoubtedly be adopted very soon after an American declaration of war. See *The Congressional Digest*, XVII, 3, March 1938, pp. 75-6.

mitted to a General Mobilization Commission (Kokka Sodoin Shingi-kai)[13] for advice before promulgation, and examination is not perfunctory. Prior to November 30, 1939, the following ordinances had been issued under the various articles of the General Mobilization Act indicated in parenthesis:[14]

General Mobilization Enterprise Designation Ordinance (Art. 3)[15]
National Conscription Ordinance (Art. 4)[16]
Factory Working Hours Limitation Ordinance (Art. 6)[17]
Employment Limitation Ordinance (Art. 6)[18]
University and School Graduates Employment Limitation Ordinance (Art. 6)[19]
Wage Control Ordinance (Art. 6) [20]
Ordinance for Emergency Regulation of Wages (Art. 6)[21]
Rice Hulling, etc. Restriction Ordinance (Art. 8)[22]
Ordinance for Control of Electric Power (Art. 8)[23]
Company Profit, Dividend, and Capital Financing Ordinance (Art. 11)[24]

[13] The *Shingi-kai* first met on August 10, 1938. See *Tokyo Asahi*, August 11, 1938, p. 137.

[14] See "Sodoin Ho Shikko Ikkanen" (One Year's Enforcement of the General Mobilization Law), *Tokyo Asahi*, June 15, 1939, p. 194. There is also a useful list of ordinances in *Trans-Pacific*, August 10, 1939, p. 19. The author believes the list given below to be complete to November 30, 1939, but the sources available do not permit complete assurance that nothing has been overlooked.

[15] *Sodoin Gyomu Shitei Rei*. Promulgated July 5, 1939. Text in *Kampo* (Official Gazette), No. 3748, pp. 130-1.

[16] *Kokumin Choyo Rei*. July 8, 1939. *Kampo*, No. 3751, pp. 321-3. For a discussion of the reasons for this ordinance and difficulties in application see Sugiyama Heisuke, "Sodoin Ho Dai Shi Jo no Hatsudo" (Invocation of Article 4 of the General Mobilization Law), *Kaizo*, XXI, 5, May 1939, pp. 214-22.

[17] *Kojo Shugyo Jikan Seigen Rei*. March 31, 1939. Abridged text in *Tokyo Asahi*, March 31, 1939, p. 410. Enforcement regulations, *ibid.*, April 19, 1939, p. 234.

[18] *Yatoiire Seigen Rei*. March 31, 1939. A summary of the provisions of the Employment Limitation Ordinance and of the Technician Training Ordinance is given in the *Japan Year Book 1939-40*, pp. 706-11. For the industries affected see *Tokyo Asahi*, April 9, 1939, p. 102.

[19] *Gakko Sotsugyo-sha Shiyo Seigen Rei*. August 24, 1938. Text in *Tokyo Asahi*, August 24, 1938, p. 316.

[20] *Chinkin Tosei Rei*. March 31, 1939. Abridged text in *Tokyo Asahi*, March 31, 1939, p. 410. Enforcement regulations, *ibid.*, April 9, 1939, p. 102.

[21] *Chinkin Rinji Sochi Rei*. October 18, 1939. *Kampo*, No. 3837, pp. 575-6.

[22] *Beikoku Tosei nado Seigen Rei*. November 25, 1939. *Kampo*, No. 3867, p. 959.

[23] *Denryoku Chosei Rei*. October 18, 1939. *Kampo*, No. 3837, pp. 581-2.

[24] *Kaisha Rieki Haito oyobi Shikin Yutsu Rei*. April 1, 1939. Text in *Tokyo Asahi*, April 1, 1939, p. 6. See also Miriam S. Farley, "Japanese Army Wins Fight to Limit Dividends," *Far Eastern Survey*, VIII, 13, June 21, 1939, pp. 153-4.

Ordinance for Emergency Regulation of the Supply of Corporate Employees (Art. 11)[25]
Factory and Workshop Supervision Ordinance (Art. 13)[26]
General Mobilization Enterprises Installations Ordinance (Art. 16)[27]
Ordinance for the Control of Prices, etc. (Art. 19)[28]
Ordinance for the Control of Ground and House Rents (Art. 19)[29]
Medical Professional Ability Registration Ordinance (Art. 21)[30]
Seamen's Vocational Ability Registration Ordinance (Art. 21)[31]
Veterinary Profession Ability Registration Ordinance (Art. 21)[32]
National Vocational Ability Registration Ordinance (Art. 21)[33]
School Technician Training Ordinance (Art. 22)[34]
Factory and Workshop Technician Training Ordinance (Art. 22)[35]
Marine Navigation Technician Training Ordinance (Art. 22)[36]
Ordinance Regarding Planning by Directors of General Mobilization Enterprises (Art. 24)[37]
General Mobilization Experiment and Research Ordinance (Art. 25)[38]
General Mobilization Indemnification Commission Regulations (Art. 29)[39]
General Mobilization Commission Ordinance (Art. 50)[40]

Many of the provisions of these ordinances have been directed toward a more efficient organization and integration of con-

[25] *Kaisha Shokuin Kyuyo Rinji Sochi Rei.* October 18, 1939. *Kampo,* No. 3837, pp. 578-80.

[26] *Kojo Jigyojo Kanri Rei.* May 4, 1938. Promulgated to replace the provisions of the *Gunju Kogyo Doin Ho* which was repealed with the enforcement of the General Mobilization Law on May 5.

[27] *Sodoin Gyomu Jigyo Setsubi Rei.* July 1, 1939. *Kampo,* No. 3745, pp. 2-3.

[28] *Kakaku nado Tosei Rei.* October 18, 1939. *Kampo,* No. 3837, pp. 573-5. For discussion see also *Trans-Pacific,* October 26, 1939, p. 22.

[29] *Jidai Yachin Tosei Rei.* October 18, 1939. *Kampo,* No. 3837, pp. 575-6.

[30] *Iryo Kankei-sha Noryoku Shinkoku Rei.* August 24, 1938. Text in *Tokyo Asahi,* August 24, 1938, p. 316.

[31] *Sen-in Shokugyo Noryoku Shinkoku Rei.* January 30, 1939.

[32] *Juishi Shokugyo Noryoku Shinkoku Rei.* February 4, 1939.

[33] *Kokumin Shokugyo Noryoku Shinkoku Rei.* January 7, 1939. Japanese text in *Tokyo Asahi,* January 7, 1939, p. 68. English summary in *The Japan Year Book, 1939-40,* pp. 712-14.

[34] *Gakko Ginosha Yosei Rei.* March 31, 1939.

[35] *Kojo Jigyojo Ginosha Yosei Rei.* April 5, 1939.

[36] *Sempaku Unko Ginosha Yosei Rei.* November 21, 1939. *Kampo,* No. 3864, pp. 829-30.

[37] *Sodoin Gyomu Jigyoshu Keikaku Rei.* July 26, 1939. *Kampo,* No. 3766, pp. 945-6.

[38] *Sodoin Shiken Kenkyu Rei.* August 30, 1939. *Kampo,* No. 3796, p. 1237.

[39] *Sodoin Hosho Iinkai Kitei.* July 2, 1938. For text and membership of the commission see *Tokyo Asahi,* July 3, 1938, p. 33.

[40] *Kokka Sodoin Shingi-kai Rei.* May 4, 1938.

trols already partially exercised under less general statutes, and, if the war continues, further invocation of the General Mobilization Law is probable.

Many other laws related directly or indirectly to national defense have been enacted since 1937, eighty-four by the 74th Diet alone. Many of these are mentioned elsewhere in this study. Of the remainder the following are most directly related to mobilization:

Law for Increase of Production of Minerals for Military Use (*Gunyo Kobutsu Zosan Ho*)
Resources Distribution Control Law (*Shiryo Haikyu Tosei Ho*)
Machine Tools Undertakings Law (*Kosaku Kikai Jigyo Ho*)
Imperial Mining Development Company Law (*Teikoku Kogyo Kaihatsu Kabushiki Kaisha Ho*)
Light Metals Manufacture Undertakings Law (*Kei Kinzoku Seizo Jigyo Ho*)
Military Horses Resources Protection Law (*Gunma Shigen Hogo Ho*)

On the whole, this Japanese war-time control, whether by separate statutes or by Imperial ordinances under the General Mobilization Act, has not gone beyond contemporary parallels in France and England or Western precedents of the World War period.[41]

5. SOCIAL WELFARE

Demands for new government activities concerned primarily with public welfare without specific connection with the promotion of one or another industry have been increasing in Japan during recent years. Their connection with national defense has already been suggested. They have also a close logical relationship to other control measures—if *laissez faire* is to be abandoned in the business field, why not even more so in the field of personal and public welfare? Welfare legislation has been advocated in the United States under the slogan of the "New Deal"—allegedly a re-definition under modern conditions of the principles of democracy on which the country was founded. The slogan is an effective one even if appeal to the constitutional fathers gives no concrete guidance as

[41] A "Table of the Wartime Economic Structure" is given in the *Tokyo Gazette*, No. 19, January 1939, pp. 25-7.

to the suitability of specific legislation today. Japanese, by a similar process, advocate welfare legislation under the slogan of *Kodo*, or the Imperial Way, which is supposed to stand for the modern application of the old principle of Imperial concern for the welfare of every subject no matter how humble. *Kodo*, too, is a seductive slogan even if, on analysis, the sayings of sage Emperors fail to give clear guidance as to whether one should vote for the Minseito or the Seiyukai.

Emergency relief for sufferers from natural calamities such as earthquakes, floods, and fires is an old story in Japan although such relief, whether through direct provision of necessities or through exemption from taxes, has been further regularized in recent years by new legislation. Through its control of the insurance business, the government has recently promoted insurance against flood, earthquake, and earthquake-fire losses and against damage to crops or small fishing vessels as measures of social welfare, providing subsidies and guarantees in cases where excessive risks would otherwise make insurance prohibitive or impossible.

From relief for earthquake sufferers it is but a step to aid for farmers impoverished by drought. The widespread suffering in the Tohoku area in 1931 and 1932 as a result of both drought and the fall of agricultural prices, for example, forced the government to appropriate considerable funds for direct relief. Next came relief for silk producers suffering from the American depression and the invention of rayon. That the causes were not natural but man-made was irrelevant. The unemployment problem in industry became severe at about the same time.

Although direct assistance and public works were resorted to, unemployment relief took a different general course in Japan than in the United States, partly because greater family solidarity and the more recent links between industrial workers and their relatives in rural regions cushioned the shock of unemployment, partly because Japan could not afford the tremendous American deficits for relief purposes, and partly because, since Japan's other recovery measures proved more effective than those in the United States, industrial expansion took up much of the slack. Economic recovery thus became the chief solution to unemployment, but it was supplemented by the encouragement of emigration, by legal provision for discharge allowances,[1] and by a national system of public employment bureaus. Special attention has been given to provision of work for discharged and wounded soldiers, their families, and the families of war dead. Since the war, of course, the problem has been primarily one of easing the transition from declining to expanding industries. Aside from this, there has been a shortage rather than a surplus of labor.

Labor legislation developed late in Japan. Its need was scarcely felt until after the Russo-Japanese War and, although the government took the initiative, it was difficult to convince the Diet and the business community of the desirability of factory regulations. The Factory Act (*Kojo Ho*) of 1911, which was not applied until five years later, provided a beginning. It was amended in 1923 to comply with some of the conventions of the International Labour Office and is supplemented by the Mining Act (*Kogyo Ho*), the Mariners Act (*Sen-in Ho*), and the Seamen's Minimum Age and Health Certificate Act (*Sen-in Saitei Nenrei Ho*).[2] The improvement of conditions, hours, and wages of labor is retarded by the low returns for labor on Japan's overcrowded farms and by the dependence of Japan's standards of living in general on the ability of her industries to compete in protected world markets. No trade union law has yet been enacted although unions are recognized *de facto*. Mediation for the settlement of labor disputes has been officially recognized since the Labor Disputes Conciliation Law (*Rodo Sogi Chotei Ho*) of 1926, and a considerable proportion of strikes are in practice settled by collective bargaining. Since the war, wages of skilled workmen, particularly in the metal trades, have risen rapidly. This has led to official control over employment and wages to prevent factories from competing for skilled workmen in a manner harmful to the mobilization program.[3] Similar measures were, of course, familiar in the West during the World War. Finally, in August 1939 a system of labor conscription was enforced under the General Mobiliza-

[1] For a cogent criticism of the 1936 statute see Goto Kiyoshi, "Taishoku Tsumitatekin oyobi Taishoku Teate Ho" (The Withdrawal from Employment Reserves and Allowance Law), *Kokka Gakkai Zasshi*, L, 8, August 1936, pp. 1008-27.

[2] See International Labour Office, *Industrial Labour in Japan* (1933), pp. 135-48.

[3] For a survey of some recent labor policies see "Current Labour Measures," *Tokyo Gazette*, No. 24, June 1939, pp. 17-26. Also "Sustenance of Labour Power in Industries," *ibid.*, III, 2, August 1939, pp. 16-22.

tion Act to provide labor for necessary undertakings in Japan and on the continent. Conscripts are compelled to serve, but they receive wages at prevailing home rates rather than military allowances.[4]

Education has profited from the popularity of social welfare legislation. Part-time education in youth schools (*seinen gakko*) has been made compulsory for all males from twelve to nineteen years of age who are not in full-time classes or military service. Application of the same system to girls has been advocated, and extension of regular compulsory education by two years (from age twelve to fourteen) has been strongly urged by successive ministers of education. This change, not yet accomplished, would bring Japan's public system of education, which is already well above that of any other Asiatic country, approximately to the level maintained in England or in the less prosperous sections of the United States.

A number of low-cost housing projects have been carried out in recent years. The shortage of building materials because of war needs makes an extensive program difficult. While Japan perhaps falls behind the United States in such expensive matters as public education and housing, she is ahead in the operation since 1927 of public pawn shops,[5] since 1938 of a People's Bank (*Shomin Kinko*) for small loans at low cost to persons with small incomes,[6] and since 1916 of a system of low-cost life insurance through the post offices.[7]

The most spectacular development since the outbreak of the war in China has been the establishment of a separate Department of Public Welfare (*Kosei-sho*) with a minister of cabinet rank at its head. The Department was organized in January 1938 but had been advocated and planned well before the Lukouchiao incident. Its most important accomplishment has been the application of the National Health Insurance Law (*Kokumin Kenko Hoken Ho*) of 1938. Health insurance for

[4] See "Calling Civilians to National Service," *Tokyo Gazette*, III, 3, September 1939, pp. 102-8.

[5] This is the date of the Public Pawn Shops Law (*Koeki Shichiya Ho*). The first such public pawn shop was established much earlier, in 1912 in Miyazaki prefecture. See Kusumi Issei, "Koeki Shichiya," *Keizaigaku Jiten*, Vol. II, pp. 817-18.

[6] By the *Shomin Kinko Ho*, passed in March 1938.

[7] By the Post Office Life Insurance Law (*Kani Seimei Hoken Ho*). For recent developments along this line see "Improvements in the Post Office Life Annuity System," *Tokyo Gazette*, III, 3, September 1939, pp. 109-14.

persons employed in industries coming under the Factory or Mining Laws had been provided as early as 1922, but the 1938 statute made insurance more generally available and is of particular importance for the rural population.[8] A bill extending insurance to the salaried classes was adopted in March 1939 (*Shokuin Kenko Hoken Ho*).[9] In the matter of medical insurance Japan is behind some European nations but ahead of most of the American States. The Department of Public Welfare has also carried on a campaign for public health, particularly against tuberculosis and venereal diseases, has regulated the prices and qualities of various drugs, has aided in the establishment of playgrounds and gymnasiums, has administered most of the relief for wounded soldiers and the families of war dead, and has had a share in the regulation of the prices of consumers' goods.

In addition to those listed in this immediate connection, many of the measures described earlier under economic recovery or agricultural security should also be associated with the problem of social welfare because relief for a distressed group in the population was at least a subsidiary motive in their enactment. In a more general sense all of the measures of economic control so far discussed are involved, for social welfare legislation depends in the long run on the ability of the national economy to support the expenditures involved.

6. FINANCE

Growth in the functions of government is impossible without an increase in personnel and expenditure, and this in turn brings greater governmental influence over the national monetary and financial system. While the number of state employees has grown in Japan, the expansion has not been so marked as, for example, in the United States under the New Deal, perhaps in part because of the effective use of private agencies in the application of new policies.[1] A considerable increase in

[8] The provisions and operation of the National Health Insurance Law are discussed in "Health Insurance for Industrial Workers," *Tokyo Gazette*, No. 14, August 1938, pp. 9-14, and "The Work of the National Health Insurance Associations," *ibid.*, No. 22, April 1939, pp. 41-3.

[9] See "Health Insurance for the Salaried Classes," *Tokyo Gazette*, No. 23, May 1939, pp. 20-4.

[1] The number of civil government employees (*bunkan*) rose from 128,792 in 1928 to 159,877 in 1937, and their total pay increased from ¥156,462,037 to ¥190,788,126 in the same period, according to the *Dai Nippon Teikoku Tokei Nenkan* (Statistical Yearbook of the Japanese Empire) for 1938, p. 434.

the civil budget has been required, however, by the increased staff, relief expenditures, and local grants in aid.

In addition, military expenditures were rapidly increased after the Manchurian incident and again, of course, after Lukouchiao. The total national budget just prior to the World War was in the neighborhood of 600 million yen; in the post-war decade it amounted to about 1,500 million yen; it grew to 4,300 million yen in 1936 and to nearly 9,000 million in 1939. This is a striking and, to some observers, an alarming increase. It is not, however, unique. The budget of the United States has climbed from 735 million dollars in 1914 to 4,000 million in 1931 and to about 10,000 million in 1939. This comparison reflects the same rate of increase, yet it neglects the tremendous budgets of the World War years which might more properly be compared with Japan's present war financing. The comparison is, of course, superficial, for it disregards such questions as national income and changing price levels. It suggests, however, that Japanese and American budgets are making the same steep climb.

Comparison of military expenditures alone gives a somewhat, but not strikingly, different result. Japan's peace-time military budget has increased at about the same rate of speed as that of the United States, Japan spending about as much in yen annually as the United States spends in dollars. At the present time, however, Japan is allocating about four to five billion yen per year to special war accounts. This increase is greater than that in the United States in 1939, since the latter is still at peace, but it is much smaller than the expansion which took place in the American war budget in the peak year of 1919 (approximately eleven billion dollars).

Since 1930 expanding military and civil expenditures have been only partly covered by increased tax receipts. The continuing deficits have been met by issuance of government bonds on the theory that while increased taxes might check recovery, prosperous business conditions will eventually make possible a natural increase in revenues.[2] The public debt has, consequently, risen rapidly: from ¥2,584,122,000 on March 31, 1914, and ¥2,579,946,000 in 1919, to ¥4,512,608,000 in 1930 and ¥17,344,852,000 in 1939. Since 1914 the American national

[2] Statements of Japanese ministers of finance in defense of this policy are strikingly similar to those of President Franklin D. Roosevelt.

debt has multiplied about thirty-seven times, that of Japan about seven times. Since 1930, however, the Japanese debt has quadrupled while that of the United States has merely tripled. Naturally many Japanese businessmen are concerned over the large deficits but, on the whole, the government still shows confidence in its ability to continue to finance the war. The treasury now markets "baby bonds" through the post-office network, but most of the issues are still disposed of through the large banks, principally the Bank of Japan.

Needless to say, the Japanese Government has given much attention to the problem of assuring the continued smooth absorption of national bonds without curtailing the capital supply necessary for the war-time program of increased production. The exchange control measures discussed above were one step in this direction. Related thereto has been the encouragement of gold and silver production and the mobilization of supplies of the precious metals. The purchase price for mined gold was raised on May 2, 1938, and on July 4, 1938, an ordinance was promulgated authorizing the purchase of gold coins for melting. In the winter of 1938-9 a national gold census was carried out, and this was extended to foreign residents in Japan the following summer. The 74th Diet authorized the creation of the Japan Gold Production Encouragement Corporation to foster gold mining still further.[3]

Legal authorization for control of investments was provided in the Emergency Capital Adjustment Law (*Rinji Shikin Chosei Ho*) of September 1937. This law permits the government to require reports from private business on the supply and movement of capital, on matters relating to securities or international receipts and payments, and on capitalization plans. It prohibits the increase of capital or the expansion of productive equipment except with official permission. It establishes an Emergency Capital Adjustment Commission (*Rinji Shikin Chosei Iinkai*) to advise the government on the application of the law (compare the Capital Issues Commission in the United States during the World War) and gives supervisory powers to the Bank of Japan. In addition, in the case of war industries the Emergency Capital Adjustment Law permits special exceptions to the limitations on stock and bond issues

[3] By the Japan Gold Production Encouragement Corporation Law (*Nippon Sankin Shinko Kabushiki Kaisha Ho*).

contained in the general corporation laws, while giving additional powers of governmental control over companies which take advantage of these exceptions. The regulations for the enforcement of this law have, of course, been changed from time to time as new problems have arisen. As in the case of foreign exchange restrictions, its first application tended seriously to hamper export industries, but subsequent modifications, made under the leadership of Ikeda Seihin, have to some extent overcome this adverse effect.

Taxation has been increased by a number of new statutes, most of them of recent date. Postal rates and tobacco monopoly prices were increased in November 1936. An excess profits tax levied on incomes benefiting from the post-1931 boom had been enacted earlier. The Temporary Tax Increase Law (*Rinji Sozei Zocho Ho*) of 1937 increased the rate of this excess profits tax and of the income tax, inheritance tax, capital interest tax, corporation income tax, mining products tax, *sake* tax, sugar consumption tax, and exchange tax.[4] The North China Affair Special Tax Law (*Hoku-Shi Jiken Tokubetsu-zei Ho*) of August 1937 further increased the rates on incomes, excess profits, and dividends, and added special commodity taxes on a few luxury articles and a tax on the interest derived from public bonds and debentures.[5] The Juridical Persons Capital Tax Law (*Hojin Shihon-zei Ho*) of 1937 levied a tax of one per mille on corporate capital.[6] The taxation of unearned incomes was further equalized by the Foreign Currency Bonds Special Tax Law (*Gaikasai Tokubetsu-zei Ho*), and a Negotiable Securities Transfer Tax Law (*Yuka Shoken Iten-zei Ho*) was applied at the same time.[7] Since 1937 the major changes have been in the direction of increases in the rates of those taxes already mentioned. None of these measures is a Japanese invention. It is worth noting, however, that they are calculated to place the burden of taxation on the groups best able to pay. The sales tax, which falls heavily on low-income groups, has been avoided. Some local taxes have been reduced and the government has increased its local grants in aid. In the past the complaint has been made that the Japanese tax system

[4] An English translation of the text is given in Sebald, *op. cit.*, pp. 75-84.
[5] English translation, *ibid.*, pp. 85-102. Japanese summary in *Tokyo Asahi*, August 3, 1937, p. 43.
[6] English translation in Sebald, *op. cit.*, pp. 103-9.
[7] Both translated, *ibid.*, pp. 111-26.

unduly burdened the rural population in comparison to urban business. Whatever the justice of this charge, it is probable that since the war the relative burden on the farmer has been reduced. Whether that burden has been reduced absolutely as well cannot be determined without complicated and highly controversial adjustments for price changes of both farm and industrial commodities.[8] Japanese tax increases are probably still inadequate, but so far there is no evidence available to show that they have not been applied at least as intelligently and with as much concern for equitable distribution of their burden as have tax increases during the last decade in the United States. The spiral of increased economic control, increased administrative costs, aggravated financial problems, and increased economic control continues upward in both countries.

[8] Shiomi Saburo, "The Incidence of Taxation upon the Rural Population under War Conditions," *Kyoto University Economic Review*, XIV, 2, April 1939, pp. 24-32. See also a table showing changes in direct and indirect taxes printed in *Trans-Pacific*, May 18, 1939, p. 19, from the *Nichi Nichi Economist*.

PART II

POLITICAL AND ADMINISTRATIVE REORGANIZATION

Even from the cursory survey which we have made it becomes obvious that the work of the Japanese Government has expanded greatly during the last decade. Today the government has a myriad duties: thousands of *kumiai*, scores of cartels, and many special corporations must be supervised; the supply, demand, and prices of hundreds of commodities must be adjusted; every significant transaction in foreign exchange must be scrutinized; elaborate reports on private or corporate business and income must be analyzed and filed; each major change in capitalization must be checked; the special competences of each laborer must be recorded, classified, and utilized; the health of each citizen must be watched more closely than ever before. These functions have not been added systematically in accordance with some great, long-range plan, but rather piecemeal and independently as different segments of the complex Japanese economic problem have become acute. As the controls of each department of the government spread further into the economic system, they soon came into conflict. The earlier, simple controls could be applied separately by such departments as those of Agriculture and Forestry or Commerce and Industry without friction, but the new controls affected economic life too closely to be so divisible. Rice is an agricultural commodity, yet its price affects Japan's export industries; fertilizer is an industrial product, yet its supply is vital to the Japanese farmer. Correlation between the policies of different bureaus becomes more essential the greater the measure of economic control exercised by each. The detailed rules under one of the General Mobilization Law ordinances had to be issued jointly by the cabinet and no less than six separate departments.[1] Changed functions also affect the relations between the administrative services, civil or military, and the legislature. Direct democracy is less workable in an era of detailed economic regulation than in former days of general

---

[1] Cited by Miyazawa Toshiyoshi in "Gyosei Kiko" (Administrative Machinery), *Kokka Gakkai Zasshi*, LIII, 9, September 1939, p. 1221.

legislation. A referendum on the proper size of cables for a suspension bridge would be just about as sensible as one on the articles of some of the new laws. These modern problems of administrative and political reorganization with which Japanese statesmen have been struggling during the last few years may be roughly classified under five headings:

a. Creation of organs for expert, long-range, nonpartisan economic planning.

b. Encouragement of executive leadership strong enough to overcome difficulties of jurisdiction and co-operation met with in the application of new measures.

c. Reorganization of executive departments and bureaus so as to secure maximum efficiency and co-ordination.

d. Reorganization of the legislature and readjustment of its relations to the executive in order to achieve the maximum participation of public opinion in government without undue sacrifice of the expert guidance necessary for economic control and planning.

e. Improvement of the means of keeping the people informed of the work of their government and of education in the social responsibilities of a less individualistic society.

1. ADMINISTRATIVE PROBLEMS

A. Expert Advisory Organs

In recent years many countries have increased their reliance on expert advisory commissions or organs of one sort or another. In the United States, investigating commissions were a favorite expedient of President Hoover and have been appointed more recently by President Roosevelt. The British road to important economic and colonial legislation has frequently been paved with reports of Royal commissions. Special economic councils have been organized in many countries. They include the Soviet *Gosplan*, the *Reichswirtschaftsrat* in Germany under the Weimar Constitution, the *Consiglio Nazionale delle Corporazioni* in Italy, and the *Conseil National Economique* in France. Japan has appointed many special commissions, temporary or permanent, many of them before the recent intensification of economic control, but she was relatively slow in introducing any permanent central organ for economic planning and advice.

The first experiments in this direction were the Resources

Council (*Shigen Shingi-kai*) and the Resources Bureau (*Shigen Kyoku*), which have already been discussed. They were limited in scope to economic matters related fairly directly to national mobilization. Their influence was considerable in this field, but it was perhaps natural that far-sighted Japanese should have advocated the creation of some organ for an all-inclusive planning of the economic program which was being adopted piecemeal and sporadically by shifting cabinets and a fluctuating Diet. European examples, particularly that of Soviet Russia, and such studies as Lewis L. Lorwin's *Advisory Economic Councils*[1] stimulated the advocacy of an "economic general staff" (*keizai sambo hombu*). It was under the influence of such arguments that in May 1935 the Okada Cabinet organized a Cabinet Inquiry Council (*Naikaku Shingi-kai*) and a Cabinet Inquiry Bureau (*Naikaku Shingi Kyoku*) to conduct continuous study of economic affairs and to advise on government economic policies. The Council was intended to include experts from business and academic circles as well as leading representatives of both major parties in the Diet. Here, however, the program struck a snag. Although the Minseito was willing to co-operate, the Seiyukai boycotted the Council as it had the Okada Cabinet, and expelled from the party those who accepted positions on it. The Inquiry Council and Bureau were not very powerful organizations. One Japanese commentator describes them as being much closer to the Economic Advisory Council set up in England by the Labor Government of Ramsay MacDonald in 1930 than to the stronger bodies on the European continent.[2] Nevertheless, many Diet members were suspicious of an executive attempt to steal their prerogatives just as the American Congress has not welcomed presidential commissions. Because of the political friction thus aroused, the Inquiry Council was abolished less than a year after its establishment. The Bureau, which was composed of experts rather than political figures, was allowed to continue to function unobtrusively.

In spite of the debacle of the Inquiry Council, neither the need nor the desire for a central economic planning body decreased. Both were expressed anew from time to time, for

[1] Washington, 1931.
[2] Tamaya Muneichiro, "Keizai Sambo Hombu" (Economic General Staff), *Keizaigaku Jiten,* Supplement, pp. 135-6.

example by Minister of Finance Baba in November 1936.[3] Professor Royama states that consolidation of the position of the Bureau was the principal object of the administrative reform proposals of the Hirota Cabinet.[4] Finally, in May 1937 under the Hayashi Cabinet the Planning Office (*Kikaku-cho*) was organized. The Planning Office took over the work and the budget of the Inquiry Bureau and was ordered to aid in the study and formulation of government economic policies and in the drafting of bills for their application.[5] Associated with it was a new Central Economic Conference (*Chuo Keizai Kaigi*) which was to outline a unified economic policy for both Japan proper and overseas areas and to aid in the drafting of bills related thereto. The Central Economic Conference met under the chairmanship of the premier and the vice-chairmanship of the president of the Planning Office.[6]

Following the outbreak of hostilities in China, the duties of the Planning Office increased and revision of its statute became desirable. Under the new regulations the name was changed to *Kikaku-in,* or Planning Board, greater unity was achieved by amalgamation of the Resources Board, and both the size and status of the organization were raised. The new president was given *shinnin* rank, the highest class in the Japanese civil service and equivalent to that of ministers of state or the head of the Manchurian Affairs Bureau (*Taiman Jimukyoku*) and above that of the chief secretary of the cabinet or the director of the Legislative Bureau. Further co-ordination was assured by the appointment of the acting vice-chairman of the Manchurian Affairs Bureau as vice-chairman of the Planning Board. The function of the Planning Board is to advise the cabinet on means for the amplification and employment of the all national resources in peace or in war; it considers and prepares opinions on bills drafted by various departments or bureaus of the government and may also draft proposed legislation itself; it is, however, a purely advisory body which can

[3] Statement to the press as reported in *Contemporary Japan*, V, 4, March 1937, p. 683.
[4] Royama Masamichi, "Die wirtschaftsrechtliche Struktur als Grundlage des japanischen Wirtschaftsaufschwungs," *Weltwirtschaftliches Archiv*, 46, 1, July 1937, pp. 78-92.
[5] *Tokyo Asahi,* April 20, 1937, p. 321; May 7, 1937, p. 114.
[6] The regulations are given in the *Tokyo Asahi*, April 20, 1937, p. 321, and the first appointments in *ibid.*, June 27, 1937, p. 452.

neither introduce legislation in the Diet nor issue ordinances; its opinions are not binding upon the government.[7]

The Planning Board, nevertheless, has undoubtedly facilitated increased co-ordination and foresight in economic planning. Its work is supplemented by that of the Manchurian Affairs Bureau (*Taiman Jimukyoku*) and of the recently established China Board (*Koa-in*—literally, "Promote Asia Board").[8] The services which these organs provide are not likely soon to be dispensed with, but further changes in their organization and powers may be expected. Their work is still in an experimental stage and, if Japan succeeds in consolidating her new position on the continent, further integration of the Planning Board, the Manchurian Affairs Bureau, and the China Board will probably become necessary.

B. *Effective Leadership*

No progress in the development of expert planning organs can eliminate the need for political leadership. Japan feels this need particularly because her government, in spite of Imperial prerogatives and the limited power of the Diet, lacks strong executive control. The Japanese premier is in a weaker position than either the president of the United States or the British prime minister. His position is more nearly that of the French premier, minus the special dictatorial powers granted to Daladier and other recent statesmen. Both depend on an unstable coalition. The coalition in Japan, however, is not primarily one of parties, although they too must be considered, but is one between a considerable number of organs and officials: the House of Representatives, House of Peers, Privy Council, each department but particularly the army and navy, and the *jushin*, or ministers close to the Throne. Each of these groups is protected in its position by the Japanese Constitution, written or unwritten, and no government can operate effectively without a working agreement with all of them. The degree of control over the cabinet which each can exercise depends even more on the support it can elicit from public opinion than

[7] See the statute of the Planning Board (*Kikaku-in Kansei*) in *Tokyo Asahi*, October 20, 1937, p. 285; October 21, 1937, p. 293.

[8] The statute of the China Board was promulgated on December 15, 1938. Its establishment, personnel and functions are discussed by Ogata Sho, "Koa-in no Shuppatsu" (The Start of the China Board), *Kaizo*, XXI, 1, January 1939, pp. 113-17.

on its somewhat vague legal powers. When in disagreement each naturally accuses the others of overstepping constitutional limits, and the cabinet gets caught in the cross-fire. This accounts for a large proportion of the political disputes of recent years, yet this very situation also makes for continuity of policy in spite of short-lived cabinets and apparent commotion: each new coalition must be very much like the last.

Faced with the difficult political problem of maintaining co-operation between these heterogeneous groups, the prime minister cannot control even his own cabinet members.[9] Each minister is constitutionally appointed by the Emperor and is responsible to him directly and individually. In December 1931 Minister of Home Affairs Adachi (a civilian member of the Diet) went on a strike to reinforce his advocacy of a coalition cabinet. He refused to resign from the Wakatsuki Cabinet yet would not attend its meetings. The premier could not force his individual resignation, and the deadlock was the immediate cause of the fall of the entire Minseito Cabinet. Even the civilian departments tend to be rather independent because of group solidarity and the strong position of the civil service. The army and navy have, in addition, the power of direct appeal to the Throne on military affairs (not including military budgets or the peace-time strength and external organization of the army), and their independence is strengthened by a provision of long standing which limits the position of minister of the army to generals or lieutenant-generals in active service and that of the minister of the navy to admirals or vice-admirals also on the active list.[10]

The prime minister must depend primarily on his national prestige and powers of persuasion to keep the coalition intact. Stable political conditions during the last thirty years have not, however, been conducive to broad national reputations like those of the *genro*, or elder statesmen, of the Meiji period, and it is difficult to find men to meet these demands. This accounts for the complaints of "weak" cabinets heard repeat-

[9] A sound summary of the historical development of the cabinet system in Japan, the problems involved, and reform proposals is given in Miyazawa Toshiyoshi, "Gyosei Kiko" (Administrative machinery), *Kokka Gakkai Zasshi*, LIII, 9, September 1939, pp. 1195-1227.

[10] A good discussion of the status of army and navy ministers appears in Kenneth Colegrove, "The Japanese Cabinet," *American Political Science Review*, XXX, 5, October 1936, pp. 903-23.

edly during the last few years. The situation has the advantage of making a personal dictatorship a practical impossibility, but it frequently leads to unfortunate delays in the adoption of necessary measures and a lack of co-ordination between the policies of different departments. The problem of how to improve central leadership without inviting dictatorship has been raised frequently. In October 1935, for example, the Cabinet Inquiry Bureau was reported to be studying measures to increase the powers of the premier. During the spring and summer of 1939, army men were reported on several occasions to be in favor of increasing the powers of the premier in order to solve the jurisdictional disputes between departments which were holding up application of the General Mobilization Law.[11] It is also interesting to recall that Nishio Suehiro, a Social Mass Party member, was expelled from the Diet on March 23, 1938, for having publicly advised the premier to "act with the boldness of a Mussolini, a Hitler, or a Stalin."[12]

Only three solutions have so far been attempted; all have been mild and only partially effective. The first has been the appointment of ministers without portfolio. In the summer of 1933 the Saito Cabinet attempted to consolidate its position by inviting the presidents of the two major parties in the House of Representatives to become ministers without portfolio, but it met with a refusal from the Seiyukai. Appointment of one or more ministers without portfolio was a prominent feature of army, cabinet, and party reform proposals following the February 26th incident. When the Hiranuma Cabinet replaced that of Prince Konoe in January 1939, and Konoe was appointed to Hiranuma's former post as president of the Privy Council, the Prince nevertheless continued to sit in the new cabinet as minister without portfolio. The propriety of this arrangement was widely questioned, but it was undoubtedly intended to strengthen the new cabinet vis-à-vis both the Privy Council and the House of Peers. The Konoe, Hiranuma, Abe, and Yonai Cabinets have all appointed emergency cabinet councillors *(rinji naikaku sangi)* from among ex-ministers and party leaders for similar reasons,[13] but lack of a clear definition of

---

[11] E.g., *Contemporary Japan*, VIII, 5, July 1939, p. 682.
[12] *Tokyo Asahi*, March 24, 1938, p. 341.
[13] For the statute governing such appointments *(Rinji Naikaku Sangi Kansei)* see the *Tokyo Asahi*, October 14, 1937, p. 189.

the duties and privileges of the councillors has led to dissatisfaction which became manifest at the time of the appointment of the Yonai Cabinet.

The second method has been the development of an inner cabinet, or five-minister conference.[14] As early as the Cabinet of Admiral Saito many important questions were practically decided by such conferences, generally composed of the premier and the army, navy, finance, and foreign affairs ministers, and the practice has re-emerged since the commencement of the war in China. It is confirmed obliquely by provision in the statute of the China Board for appointment of the premier as president of that board and of the ministers of foreign affairs, finance, army, and navy as vice-presidents. This policy of an inner cabinet is not yet old enough to have become a fixed tradition, and, in addition, the strength of the precedent is in one way lessened by the fact that other combinations of ministers have occasionally been used in similar fashion to settle other types of problems. It is not impossible, however, that in time a system will develop similar to that obtaining in England where the cabinet is in theory merely a committee of the Privy Council, and there are many ministers who do not enjoy cabinet rank.

The third step was taken on September 29, 1939 by the issuance of an ordinance requiring each minister of state, the governor-general of Korea, the governor-general of Formosa, the Japanese ambassador to Manchukuo, the governor of Saghalien, and the governor of the South Sea Islands to consult with the premier before issuing, revising, or repealing any order relating to the enforcement of the General Mobilization Law, and also authorizing the premier to give instructions on such matters.[15] This measure is intended to eliminate

[14] Compare the use of this inner cabinet and of ministers without portfolio with the British War Cabinet under Lloyd George. The British example is cited by one Japanese publicist who advocated a Japanese "war cabinet" composed of the ministers of the army, the navy, finance, foreign affairs, commerce and industry, and education. Urabe Hyakutaro, "Ika ni Naikaku Seido wo Kyoka seshimubeki ya" (How Should We Strengthen the Cabinet System?), *Gaiko Jiho (Revue Diplomatique)*, LXXXIX, 1, January 1, 1939, pp. 85-100.

[15] *Kokka Sodoin Ho nado no Shikko no Tokatsu ni kansuru Ken*. Text in *Kampo*, No. 3823, p. 1081. See also *Trans-Pacific*, September 28, 1939, p. 9, and October 5, 1937, pp. 25-6 for discussion. This ordinance was not unprecedented. The premier had been given similar powers in regard to the Munitions Industries Mobilization Law in 1920, according to Miyazawa Toshiyoshi, "Gyosei Kiko," *Kokka Gakkai Zasshi*, LIII, 9, September 1939, p. 1222.

jurisdictional disputes and may in time materially strengthen the premiership which remains today one of the weak spots in Japanese political organization.[16]

C. Reorganization of Executive Departments

No government could efficiently administer so many new functions without reorganizing many of its subordinate bureaus. The details of such adjustments are not of great significance, however. A list of the new bureaus within various departments will be sufficient to give an impression of the degree of change.

Supervising Department	New Agencies
Cabinet	Planning Board
	Manchurian Affairs Board
	Information Bureau
	Tohoku Bureau
	Personnel Bureau
	National General Mobilization Commission
	China Affairs Board
Foreign Affairs	America Bureau
	Research Department
Home Affairs	Planning Bureau
Finance	Exchange Bureau
	National Savings Bureau
Agriculture and Forestry	Rice Bureau
	Horse Administration Bureau
	Economic Rehabilitation Bureau
Commerce and Industry	Insurance Bureau
	Fuel Bureau
	Control Bureau
Communications	Control Bureau

In addition, the Department of Public Welfare is new although some of its functions were transferred from other departments. There have been proposals from time to time for the abolition of the Department of Overseas Affairs and for the creation of separate departments for foreign trade,[17]

[16] One leading student of Japanese institutions has advocated strengthening of cabinet unity, responsibility, and power by re-institution of the pre-constitutional practice of holding cabinet meetings in the Imperial presence. Nakano Tomio, "Kempo to Seiji no Kyoka" (The Constitution and the Strengthening of Politics), *Chuo Koron*, LIV, 8, August 1939, pp. 4-19.

[17] See Kimpara Kennosuke, "Boeki-sho Ron" (On a Department of Trade), *Kaizo*, XXI, 12, November 1939, pp. 65-71.

for labor, or for Chinese affairs. Mergers, notably that of the Departments of Commerce and Industry and of Agriculture and Forestry have also been mentioned. The actual changes have, however, been small in comparison to the avalanche of new legislation, and it will not be surprising if many more such adjustments are made during the next few years.[18]

2. LEGISLATURE AND EXECUTIVE

No cabinet composed primarily of members of a party in the House of Representatives has held office in Japan since May 1932. Although the importance of this fact can be easily exaggerated, no survey of modern Japanese governmental changes would be complete without consideration of its causes. That the Japanese cabinet must be a coalition between different groups and that the influence of each group depends to a considerable measure on public opinion have already been suggested. For a few years following the promulgation of the Japanese Constitution the major parties in the House of Representatives were excluded from representation in the cabinet. It was soon discovered, however, that this prevented effective operation of the constitutional system, and since about 1896 every cabinet, with one or two unsuccessful exceptions, has sought a working agreement with the Diet. This did not mean that the Diet was given control of either the composition or the policies of the cabinet; it was merely admitted to participation in the coalition. Such an arrangement is consistent with the provisions in the Japanese Constitution and with Japanese precedent. The parties, like other groups, sought to extend their influence and found support for their efforts in Western theories of constitutional government which assume, probably uncritically, that development toward full parliamentary control is a necessary or at least the "normal" path of political evolution. Post-War trends in other parts of the world were conducive to such opinions and, for a few years, principally from 1924 to 1932, party cabinets ruled Japan. Their control was never complete, however, for the traditional position of the civil and military services, the Privy Council, and the

[18] On needs for the further unification of administration see the short statement by Matsukata Kojiro, "Tosei Ichigen Ka no Kyumu" (The Urgency of Unification of Control), *Chuo Koron,* LIV, 5, May 1939, pp. 352-3.

House of Peers could not be violated without recrimination and retaliation.

The course of Japanese politics during the late 1920's was punctuated by a series of clashes between the cabinet and the other organs of the government, ostensibly over such questions as financial aid to banks in the panic of 1927, the issuance of amendments to the Peace Preservation Law (*Chian Iji Ho*) in the guise of an emergency ordinance, certain phrases in the Pact for the Renunciation of War, or the ratification of the London Naval Treaty. Each also represented a protest against the attempt to alter radically the political balance of power in favor of the parties in the House of Representatives at the expense of the peers, the Privy Council, the civil and military services and the *jushin*. The parties might have carried the day had they enjoyed genuine popular confidence. Instead it was common knowledge that bribery in elections was the rule rather than the exception and that party leaders depended on big business for the millions of yen necessary for each political campaign. Interference with elections through the party-controlled Department of Home Affairs was so common that it was said the government in power never lost an election. Corrupt deals between government officials and private interests were frequently rumored and occasionally exposed. The parties were therefore vulnerable to the countercharges of the non-elected organs whose share in cabinet control they were attempting to reduce.

The world depression and events connected therewith spelled failure for the party campaign, at least for the present. Economic collapse weakened the prestige of Western social theories. Japanese who had advocated greater powers for the legislature on the strength of Western experience found their arguments contradicted by a Western swing toward greater executive powers. Nationalism, resurgent in Japan as everywhere else, reinforced the arguments of those who wished to preserve the customary balance in political life. Growing recognition of the economic character of national defense and the Manchurian incident increased the prestige and widened the legitimate concern of the professional military services. Crisis conditions, both economic and diplomatic, plus European precedents, led to demands for a moratorium on partisan strife and for the establishment of a coalition cabinet. In short, everything conspired to weaken the party campaign against the prerogatives of the other governmental organs. When the tottering Wakatsuki Cabinet fell in December 1931 as a result of the advocacy of a coalition by one of its own members, it was already clear that, in the absence of far-reaching political reforms, no new party cabinet would have much hope for long life. It was reported that the *genro*, Prince Saionji, before nominating Inukai for the premiership, had warned the latter of the serious situation and had inquired whether he was confident of his ability to control it. Inukai was similarly warned by the usually liberal *Asahi* newspaper.[1] The Seiyukai Cabinet, born under the cloud of exchange speculation, was criticized for failure to resign in acceptance of responsibility for an attempt on the life of the Emperor (the Sakuradamon affair of January 8, 1932),[2] and lost prestige with the assassinations of Inoue Junnosuke (February 9, 1932) and Baron Dan (March 5, 1932). A reform program would perhaps not have stemmed the tide, but even this the Seiyukai Cabinet did not have. When the premier was assassinated on May 15, 1932, party cabinets, which had ruled at best for but a decade or so, came to an end, and Japan returned again to the earlier system of a coalition wider in scope than the groups in the House of Representatives.

The parties were still recognized, however. Since 1932 the major parties have been openly condemned only by the short-lived Hayashi Cabinet.[3] All other cabinets have welcomed party co-operation and limited party representation. Yonai has welcomed the president of the Minseito into his cabinet. At the same time each cabinet has urged political reforms to aid in the rehabilitation of the Diet in public opinion.[4]

The most successful of these has been the revision of the

[1] *Tokyo Asahi,* January 3, 1932, p. 3.

[2] The *Tokyo Asahi* (January 10, 1932, 10-17) scathingly denounced the Seiyukai's "not yet sated lust for power."

[3] Only two of the eleven cabinets which Japan has had during the last ten years have been headed by generals—those of Hayashi in 1937 and Abe in 1939. It is interesting to note, therefore, that the China policy of the Hayashi Cabinet was somewhat more liberal than that of its predecessors and that the Cabinet also sought a *rapprochement* with Great Britain. See Arnold J. Toynbee, *Survey of International Affairs, 1937,* London, 1938, Vol. I, pp. 162-8.

[4] For a useful summary of proposals for reform of the Diet see Yabe Tadaharu, "Gikai Seido" (The Diet System), *Kokka Gakkai Zasshi,* LIII, 9, September 1939, pp. 1161-94.

election law. Manhood suffrage was granted in 1925. Woman suffrage is still remote although it is likely to be hastened by the increasing employment of women in business and industry during the present war. Accordingly, extension of the franchise has not been a primary issue during the last decade. The election law revision of 1934 was planned instead to curtail bribery and, by reducing the cost of elections, to facilitate the representation of minorities and the poorer classes. At one time the government favored full-fledged proportional representation, but, as a result of opposition in the Diet, it compromised instead on the system of the single vote in plural-member constituencies. While this system does not result in full proportionality, it does assure representation in the Diet to any group which can poll about one-fifth of the vote in a given constituency and which has the unity and good sense to limit its candidates in proportion to its strength. In addition, the new law radically limits election expenses (to about ten thousand yen per candidate but varying somewhat with the size of the constituency) and the size of campaign organizations. It provides for free distribution by the post office of one statement of qualifications and platform by each candidate to every elector in his constituency but prohibits further canvassing by mail. It greatly increases the penalties for irregular use of election funds. By providing a limited degree of proportional representation and curtailing the advantages of wealth in election campaigns, the revised election law has been primarily responsible for the increased number of proletarian and independent members in the Diet. Were American election laws equally favorable to minorities, there would probably be both socialists and communists in Congress today. Recent governments have also stopped partisan police interference with elections and have sponsored a national campaign for election reform and for education designed further to check bribery and to increase the ratio of voters to those holding the franchise.

The election law does not directly diminish party influence. In fact, in some ways it gives the established parties an added advantage, for it places no limitations on party campaigns as long as they are general in nature and not specifically directed toward aiding a single candidate. This is typical of the policy of recent governments which have never fully succumbed to the many demands for the establishment of a single official party as in Italy, Germany, or the Soviet Union. Such a single party was advocated by Adachi in 1931, by Matsuoka in 1933, by Toyama Mitsuru and his associates in December 1938, and by the *Shakai Taishu-to* and the *Toho-kai* (proletarian parties) on various occasions from 1937 to 1939. It has been repeatedly discussed by individual cabinet ministers. General Hayashi seemed on the verge of undertaking its organization in the spring of 1937 but thought better of the project. In spite of such widespread demand for a single official party and the example of the *Kyowa-kai*, or Concordia Society, in Manchukuo, it now appears unlikely that such an organization will be sponsored by the government. Both Premier Konoe and Premier Hiranuma repeatedly stated that the government has no intention of destroying the parties and that it recognizes them as an essential part of the operation of an elective legislature. There seems to be a growing emphasis on the Constitution in discussions of the *kokutai*, or national polity, and such emphasis is inimical to drastic parliamentary reorganization.[5]

The upper chamber of the Japanese Diet, as well, has been similarly criticized. Its statute (the *Kizoku-in-rei*) had already been revised in 1925, but the reforms accomplished at that time were disappointing to their sponsors. During the so-called era of party cabinets there was a sustained campaign for emasculation of the House of Peers as part of the struggle by the House of Representatives for supremacy in the government. (The two houses of the Japanese Diet, like the House of Representatives and the Senate in the United States, enjoy approximately equal legislative and budgetary powers.) This campaign failed for reasons already suggested, and since 1932 attention has been directed to changes in the composition and organization of the upper chamber rather than in its powers. The chief proposals have been a reduction in the number of hereditary seats, a compulsory age of retirement, the abolition of the group of members now elected from among the highest taxpayers in each prefecture, and the substitution of some form of occupational representation. Behind these, usually unexpressed for political

[5] See, for example, Satomi Iwao, "Ikkoku Itto no Kokutai-gaku-teki Hihan" (Criticism of the Principle of a Single Party from the Point of View of Study of the National Policy), in *Chuo Koron* (Central Review), LIV, 1, January 1939, pp. 76-84; Sasa Hiroo, "Kokumin Soshiki Mondai no Kento" (Study of the Problem of National Organization), *ibid.*, pp. 30-40.

reasons, there has also been a desire to reform the internal unofficial political organization through which the House is dominated by a single clique—the *Kenkyu-kai*. These proposals have been directed toward meeting the charges of superannuation and oligarchical control made against the peers, toward an increase in the value of the upper house in the consideration of new national legislation, and so toward the rehabilitation in public opinion of this half of the legislature.

The campaign for reform of the House of Peers has been continuous since 1925. The need for reform has been urged by groups both outside and inside the House itself. Prince Konoe actively sponsored the reform movement while first a member and later president of the House of Peers. When he became premier, he made reform of the House a major plank in his platform. Committees and commissions for the study of reform measures are almost too numerous to name. In spite of all this agitation, nothing has been accomplished beyond somewhat greater circumspection in the exercise of their influence by the directors of the *Kenkyu-kai*. The Ordinance of the House of Peers has not been touched. The most natural time for effective reforms was prior to the new elections to the House of Peers which took place in July 1939 and, as members enjoy seven-year terms, it now appears as though reform would be indefinitely delayed.

The government and the Diet System Inquiry Commission (appointed in June 1938), having thus far failed in any notable reform of the composition of either the upper or lower chamber, have turned their attention instead to minor modifications in the Law of the Houses (*Giin-ho*) which provides for the convocation, term, dissolution or adjournment, and procedure of the Diet. Only one change has been accomplished. This extends the fixed period allowed for discussion of the budget from twenty-one to twenty-five days in each house. This change, as far as it goes, increases the possibility of effective Diet supervision over the government. The Hayashi Cabinet announced in March 1937 that subsequent regular sessions of the Diet would, when practicable, be convoked in November instead of in December in order to permit fuller consideration of legislation, but this innovation has not yet been put into practice. In addition, proposals have been made for the establishment of standing committees of the two houses which could meet between sessions of the Diet and thus make continuous the now intermittent participation of the legislature in governmental activities. This system has been opposed by the government and has not as yet become a reality.

The Diet has obviously been able to check every move for any radical change in its composition or powers. One of its chief weapons has been a counterattack on weak points in the civil and military services. Thanks to the acumen and political ability of Field Marshal Yamagata, Japan has for some forty years enjoyed most of the features of a modern administrative civil service which have recently been advocated for the United States by President Roosevelt's Committee on Administrative Reorganization. Lately, however, there has been a trend in England, the United States, and Japan to question some aspects of the civil service program, particularly the effects on efficiency and initiative of rigid civil service guarantees of tenure. The unusual influence of civil servants in Japan has given such arguments added cogency, and they have recently been exploited to the full in the Japanese Diet.[6] Administrative reforms were promised by the Konoe Cabinet and studied during the spring, summer, and fall of 1938. After the installation of the Hiranuma Cabinet, the Seiyukai and Minseito threatened to adopt a resolution providing for civil service reforms (in the direction of curtailment of civil service privileges) but were finally dissuaded from doing so. Hiranuma defended the civil servants (he was one himself) and acceded to Diet demands only to the extent of addressing a memorandum to all civil servants, admonishing them to greater endeavor, impartiality, and humility.[7] Criticism of the civil service has, however, stimulated cabinet ministers to more continuous efforts in the direction of improvement of personnel administration in the various departments, notably in the Department of Foreign Affairs.

The army and navy present a special problem although they are, of course, in much the same situation as the civil services.

[6] For a discussion of the popular grounds for criticism see Nagaoka Ryuichiro, "Kanryo no Konjaku" (Bureaucracy Past and Present), *Chuo Koron*, LIV, 3, March 1939, pp. 151-9. See also Shimizu Cho, "Kanri Seido no Kaisei ni Kansuru Kanken" (Views on the Reform of the Civil Service System), *Kokka Gakkai Zasshi*, LI, 8, pp. 1025-39; Yanase Ryokan, "Kanri Seido" (The Civil Service), *ibid.*, LIII, 9, September 1939, pp. 1228-60.

[7] The text of this circular will be found in *Tokyo Asahi*, February 25, 1939, p. 332.

The tenure of military officers is even more protected than that of other state officials. Their political influence has increased more markedly during the last decade, and their record has been marred by a number of instances of participation by active or reserve officers in assassinations or in conspiracies against important statesmen. The military services are still extremely jealous of their independent position under the supreme command and their freedom from political influences. Post-World-War emphasis on the wider meaning of national defense has, however, led officers to concern themselves with an ever wider range of political questions. The resultant increase in internal disputes over policy coincided with a decrease in the unity of principles and control due to the deaths of the *genro* Yamagata and Oyama and to the displacement of clan leadership by new men trained since the Sino-Japanese War.

Theoretically, the army and navy are under direct Imperial command, but their actual administration has been divided among several officers each of whom enjoys the privilege of direct report to the sovereign. This situation was tolerable as long as unity was maintained by the authority of the *genro*, but caused trouble when that authority disappeared. A conflict in 1931 within the army "big three"—the minister of the army, the chief of staff, and the inspector-general of military education—led to the appointment in 1932 of a member of the Imperial Family, Prince Kan-in, as chief of staff to serve as an arbiter. Friction between Minister of the Army Hayashi and Inspector-General of Military Education Mazaki over personnel policies led to the forced resignation of the latter in 1935 and was indirectly connected with the assassination of Major-General Nagata in August of that year and with the assassinations of February 26, 1936 (of which the new inspector-general of military education, Watanabe, was a victim). A somewhat similar problem in the navy was evident in 1929 when the minister and the chief of staff disagreed over the ratification of the London Naval Treaty. There was thus a double problem for both the army and the navy—a proper adjustment of relations with the cabinet and the Diet and a unification of internal control. Neither aspect of the problem could be solved except by a process of political adjustment: no formula was immediately applicable. As a result, the recent course of the army and navy in Japanese politics has not been entirely consistent. Nevertheless, the main lines are tolerably clear. The development in the navy has been less spectacular than that in the army, which may be taken as an example for both. Army leadership has, particularly since 1936, been concentrated increasingly in the hands of the minister of the army who has assumed full control of personnel shifts.[8] Continuity in the personnel and political policies of the Department has been strengthened by a return to the earlier limitation of the position of minister to generals or lieutenant-generals in *active service*, excluding those on the reserve list like General Ugaki.[9] Army officers have been prohibited from publicly expressing views on political affairs, and since February 26, 1936, those involved in illegal activities have been dealt with most severely. The Reservists' Association (*Zaigo Gunjin Kai*) has also been brought under the control of the Department.[10] The army has thus recognized that irresponsible political agitation by military officers cannot be permitted. The converse of this recognition is that the political voice of the army is concentrated in the minister of the army whose influence in the cabinet has consequently increased.

What then is the legitimate sphere of influence of the service ministers? The position which General Terauchi and subsequent ministers of the army have tried to maintain is that while the army, under modern conditions of national defense, cannot be indifferent to general economic and political problems, will express its views through the minister of the army, and reserves the right to refuse to co-operate with any cabinet not showing a proper understanding of such problems, the army will, nevertheless, not attempt to dictate either specific policies or the details of their application. These are the proper functions of the civilian branches. This distinction between readiness to block cabinets in which it lacks confidence and avoidance of interference with non-military legislation and administration is a very narrow one, and its practical application leaves much room for dissatisfaction on both sides. It amounts, however, only

[8] *Tokyo Asahi,* July 28, 1936, p. 395.
[9] *Ibid.,* May 18, 1936, p. 250. The change was purely precautionary since no officer not in active service had ever served as minister of the army or navy, even though their appointment had been possible since 1913.
[10] By ordinances promulgated on September 25, 1936. *Ibid.,* September 20, 1936, p. 278; September 26, 1936, p. 359.

to reaffirmation of the customary share of the services in the Japanese political coalition. During recent years the minister of the army has advocated many types of legislation—control of the power industry, agrarian relief, organization of a national welfare department, reform of the House of Peers, and a general mobilization act, to mention only a few. Yet none of these has been dictated. Some remain unaccomplished; others have been adopted only after formulation and debate by the civilian ministries, extended discussion in the Diet, and frequent amendments. The influence of the army and navy departments on domestic legislation and administration has increased during the last decade, but not to the point of dictatorship.

Army influence in continental policy is a different problem and one which cannot be fully examined here. Obviously the army controls Japanese activities in Manchuria and in China to a far greater extent than it does domestic affairs. This power on the continent is based on various factors: the right of direct appeal to the Throne, the special position of the Kwantung Army under the South Manchuria Railway Concession and the Kwantung Peninsula lease, the regulation of Sino-Japanese affairs since 1932 and 1933 by military truce instead of diplomatic treaty, and the existence of military hostilities since 1937. The beginnings of a compromise similar to that in Japan proper can, however, be seen in the growing integration of domestic and overseas policies discussed above and in the establishment of such organs as the Manchurian Affairs Bureau and the China Board.

Altogether the Japanese political coalition—the House of Representatives, House of Peers, Privy Council, ministers close to the Throne, army, navy, civil services—has not been radically altered during the last decade. The House of Representatives has lost influence but has retained all of its legal powers and has benefited from some reforms. Its influence would probably grow once more if its major parties could iron out their own domestic disputes which have recently made a very bad impression.[11] The Privy Council continues as before an important check on cabinet actions between sessions of the

[11] The Seiyukai in particular has been torn by petty factional disputes. During 1939 the police on several occasions had to intervene to prevent physical violence between two factions barricaded on separate floors of the party headquarters in Tokyo.

Diet.[12] The House of Peers remains approximately unchanged in both legal powers and influence. The ministers close to the Throne have probably somewhat declined in day-by-day influence, but they retain a voice in the appointment of new cabinets, and so continue to furnish indirect guidance of political developments. The army and navy have increased their influence but have also carried out internal reforms which seem to assure somewhat more responsible exercise of their powers than during the early 1930's. The civil services, too, have gained in strength but not decisively. In general, the power of the administrative branch of the government has increased while that of the legislature has decreased, but this is a universal phenomenon. The increasing rôle of national defense considerations in governmental decisions is not peculiar to Japan.

3. EDUCATION, INFORMATION, AND PROPAGANDA

Modern theories of national defense emphasize morale and, consequently, the state's concern with education and information. There are, however, other reasons why such concern inevitably accompanies increasing governmental control of business. For example, the individual feels the pressure of his government more than ever before and blames it for each of those economic maladjustments which formerly were attributed to fate or the relentless wheel of economic law. At the same time the complexities and technicalities of modern economic legislation make comprehension and legislative participation by the individual increasingly difficult. Nevertheless, the understanding and co-operation of the individual is more necessary than ever before, because the more intimately national legislation touches everyday life the less effective rigid enforcement of meticulously drafted terminology becomes; more and more depends on flexible application by semi-voluntary agencies in every hamlet, ward, or valley. The individual directly and the state indirectly have therefore become more vulnerable than ever before to ideologies which plausibly attack the established order, whatever it may be. Under such circumstances education of the people about their government and its functions and about their relations to it is certainly legitimate. At least, each

---

[12] The best discussion of the Privy Council in English is in Kenneth Colegrove, "The Japanese Privy Council," *American Political Science Review*, XXV, 3 and 4, August and November 1931.

nation has acted on that assumption. Yet the distinction between education and propaganda is a vague and subjective one at best. What sort of a balance between the two has Japan achieved?

The educational system proper has probably improved during the last decade. Preparations have been made for an extension of the term of compulsory education by two years, to the age of fourteen. Many new vocational schools and two additional Imperial universities, Osaka and Nagoya, have been opened. The national government has increased its grants in aid to local education. Co-education has been introduced at Meiji and Waseda, two of the most important private universities.

Increased support has also meant increased control, however, and there have been a number of sensational incidents over the issue of academic freedom. The expulsion of the legal historian and criminologist Takikawa in March 1933 almost wrecked the faculty of law at Kyoto Imperial University.[1] More recently serious dissension in the faculty of economics at Tokyo Imperial University has caused the expulsion of a number of professors. By far the most famous case, however, was that of Professor Emeritus Minobe, who was forced to resign from the House of Peers, narrowly escaped assassination, and was threatened with a criminal indictment because of views on the location of sovereignty which he had published with impunity, if not without criticism, some thirty years before. The same issue caused the resignation of the chief of the cabinet's Legislative Bureau and was related to that of the Lord Privy Seal, Ikki. It led to official statements by the premier and an official publication by the Department of Education on the true meaning of the national polity. Partly as a result of such incidents the Department of Education has recently reasserted its right to appoint the presidents and faculties of Imperial universities, powers until recently exercised by the faculties through university senates. So far, however, that control has been exercised with reserve, and the Imperial university faculties probably still enjoy an autonomy in administrative matters greater than that of their academic colleagues in most state universities in other countries.

The government has also extended its efforts at education

[1] See Moriguchi Shigeji, "Academic Freedom and the Takikawa Case," *Kaizo*, July 1933, translated in *Contemporary Japan*, II, 2, September 1933, pp. 327-30.

through various organizations of a less official character such as the Reservists' Association already mentioned, the *Seinendan*, or Young Men's Associations, the local autonomy movement (*chiho jichi undo*), and the Central League for Election Purification (*Senkyo Shukusei Chuo Remmei*). Government publications have increased in volume although not as spectacularly as in the United States under the New Deal; among the most significant new serials is the *Shu-ho*, or Weekly Bulletin, issued by the Cabinet Information Bureau. Most of the new publications do not call for comment, but a few, like the Department of Education volume on the *True Meaning of the National Polity*,[2] the various army and navy pamphlets, and the recent booklet on *Japan's Diplomacy* issued by the Department of Foreign Affairs,[3] are more nearly political propaganda in the generally accepted sense.

Control of "dangerous thoughts" has much the same meaning for Japanese that control of "un-American activities" has for citizens of the United States. The psychology is similar but the geography different. The geographical relation between the Soviet Union and Japan is similar to that between Canada and the United States, but the Asiatic frontier, unlike the American one, is heavily fortified, and the Russo-Japanese War is a century more recent than the War of 1812. As a result, fear of communism is much more intense in Japan than it is in the United States, and the communist party has been proscribed for some years.[4] Since 1927 there have been repeated police roundups of suspected reds, the latest of which occurred since the outbreak of hostilities in China. Concurrently there has been extensive censorship of leftist literature under the same Peace Preservation Law (*Chian Iji Ho*). This censorship has been directed primarily at publications of a popular and inflammatory nature; there has been no general proscription of scholarly works on social subjects, although the police and customs officers have frequently interpreted their duties very liberally.

Subversive activities under the cloak of patriotism have been more difficult to deal with, although they, too, threaten Japa-

[2] *Kokutai no Hongi*, Tokyo, 1937.
[3] *Nippon no Gaiko*.
[4] It is worth recalling that the communist party was proscribed in France in 1939 as soon as the Russo-German non-aggression agreement made the Soviet Union seem more of an enemy than a friend.

nese political stability. The perpetrators of the early assassinations in Japan, i.e., those of Premier Hamaguchi, Inoue Junnosuke, Baron Dan, and Premier Inukai, were treated with great leniency by the Department of Justice. They were given ample opportunities to plead their cases before the courts and public opinion. In spite of admitted guilt, their sentences were remarkably light: in Japanese tradition patriotism is the weightiest of extenuating circumstances. Even the assassin of Major-General Nagata was allowed to preach at length from the defendant's box at his court-martial. In the meantime there had, however, been some attempt by the Departments of Home Affairs and of Justice to curb the spread of violence perpetrated under the cloak of patriotism. In 1935 thousands of patriotic gangsters were rounded up all over the country. *Omotokyo,* a Shinto sect which had close connections with the Black Dragon Society, was suppressed in December 1935 on charges of lese majesty. In the following spring another such sect, *Hito-no-michi,* was proscribed. The insurrection of February 26, 1936 demonstrated the seriousness of the situation and caused an abrupt stiffening in the official attitude. Trials were held in camera to check their use for propaganda purposes. The officers responsible for the assassinations were tried and quickly executed. Aizawa, the assassin of Nagata, who had been treated so leniently before, was retried in secret and executed. Even the civilians who had helped to plan the insurrection, but had not participated in the assassinations, were sentenced and executed, including Kita Ikki, one of the best-known leaders among the secret societies. Since 1936 there has been little doubt of the intention of the government to deal with equal severity with subversive activities from whatever direction they may come. This does not mean, of course, that all patriotic societies should be disbanded. There are good and bad societies, and the Japanese Government, like the American, must show legal justification for arrests. In view of Japan's international position, the wording of the Peace Preservation Law, and the fact that a state of war exists, those who advocate the abolition of private property, pacifism, or the overthrow of the Emperor are bound to find themselves in more trouble than those who merely condemn the government of the day for malfeasance in office or for unsuccessful diplomacy.

The press and the radio have been placed under some control. Radio broadcasting emanates from the Japan Broadcasting Association which, like the British Broadcasting Company, is a public corporation and enjoys a monopoly. This system has the advantage of eliminating commercial advertisements from the air and the disadvantage of limiting broadcasting of news to that approved by the government and of almost prohibiting discussion of controversial political questions. Charges of use of the radio by the cabinet in power to promote its own political future have not been entirely lacking but, on the whole, officials have been careful not to employ the radio for partisan ends. The advantage accruing to particular statesmen in the cabinet from state operation of broadcasting is probably little greater than that enjoyed by the president of the United States through free access to radio time at his convenience over the private networks. As in England, broadcasting is supported not by advertising but by a standard charge collected monthly from each owner of a radio set. The conflict of interest over the use of news between the radio, the news agencies, and the press has been avoided by making the Broadcasting Association a member of Domei and a heavy contributor to its expenses.

The *Domei Tsushin-sha*, or United News Company, was organized with official encouragement in 1936 through the merger of *Rengo* and *Nippon Dempo*, the two earlier news agencies which corresponded roughly to the Associated Press and the United Press in the United States. The new Domei more nearly resembles the British Reuters agency or the French Havas, which it was designed to emulate. It is another example of state-sponsored monopoly but, in addition to economy and better coverage of foreign news, the merger was also designed to facilitate control of news distribution in Japan and abroad. Conflicting press releases have served to emphasize contradictions in policy between various branches of the Japanese Government, and it was hoped that the bad impression thus given could be minimized by the centralization of news distribution. More recently the government has sought to achieve the same end by restricting statements to the press to the highest officials in each department and by the organization of an Information Bureau under the cabinet (*Naikaku Joho-bu*). The latter may, in time, develop into a full-fledged ministry of propaganda such as has long operated in Germany and has recently been established in Britain. For the time being, however, information control in Japan has not progressed much beyond a limited negative censorship.

Police bans on news of criminal matters have long been applied in Japan in order to aid law-enforcing agencies by curtailing information to law breakers while investigations or arrests are under way. Such bans have frequently been abused, particularly in arrests of suspected radicals: on many occasions the newspapers have not been permitted to divulge news of large-scale arrests until more than a year after they have occurred.[5] The Department of Home Affairs may also suppress or censor books, articles, or entire numbers of periodicals considered harmful to morals or, under the Peace Preservation Law, to public peace. The latter clause covers the many leftist articles or books which have been banned or mutilated. In addition, the Department of Foreign Affairs may issue press bans on material likely to be harmful to Japan's international relations: this power was used about 1935 to stem the tide of books predicting a naval war between Japan and the United States. The army and navy have always been able to ban publication of information on troop movements and other strictly military matters, but this power has been extended to many types of information on natural resources and factory production by the Military Resources Secrets Protection Law (*Gunyo Shigen Himitsu Hogo Ho*) of 1939.[6] There is also a considerable amount of more or less voluntary self-censorship by the press under present war conditions, as there is in England. It is worth noting, however, that the bill for control of seditious literature (*Fuon Bunsho Rinji Torishimari Ho*),[7] sponsored by the Hirota Cabinet in 1936 primarily to control such incendiary pamphlets as appeared prior to the February 26th incident, was passed by the Diet only after it had been amended to apply solely to illegal documents not coming under the newspaper or publication laws. An amendment strengthening the Military Secrets Protection Law (*Gunki Hogo Ho*), which the cabinet introduced in the 70th Diet early in 1937, was not approved until after the actual outbreak of hostilities in August, two sessions

---

[5] The injustice to the defendant involved in such situations is not due primarily to any political bias but rather to the adoption in Japan of French criminal law which does not include the Anglo-Saxon writ of *habeas corpus*.

[6] See *Trans-Pacific*, July 6, 1939, p. 36.

[7] For a discussion of the law see Tanaka Jiro, "Fuon Bunsho Rinji Torishimari Ho ni tsuite," *Kokka Gakkai Zasshi*, L, 8, August 1936, pp. 1028-40.

later.[8] Many other official statements and debates in the Diet since 1937 indicate that freedom of speech is still a live issue.

Americans, who, in spite of criminal syndicalism laws, still enjoy very wide freedom of speech, would be dissatisfied with many of Japan's recent policies; but in her control of education, information, and propaganda Japan has not gone so far as Germany, Italy, or the Soviet Union. Her position today more nearly parallels that of Great Britain and France under similar war conditions with, perhaps, some greater measure of freedom for foreign correspondents in Japan.

[8] This law and German, French, English, American, Italian, and Soviet parallels are discussed at length by Hidaka Minoo, *Gunki Hogo Ho* (The Military Secrets Protection Law), Tokyo, 1937.

PART III
CONCLUSIONS

The late Justice Holmes of the United States Supreme Court used to insist that it was both expedient and constitutional that the individual states in the American Union should be permitted a wide degree of latitude in experimentation with social and economic legislation, even when the resultant policies seemed unwise or impracticable to him or to other justices. Common sense demands that any evaluation of the internal measures adopted by foreign governments be based on at least an equal degree of tolerance. It is inconceivable that two independent governments should be identical in structure or in operation. Japan has peculiarities enough to mislead the average Western observer. When these are understood, however, it becomes evident that in domestic politics Japanese statesmen seek the same advantages for their people as do Western leaders for theirs, and that this search has led them along paths not unlike those chosen in the United States, Great Britain, France, or other Western countries. The factors directing the course selected are world-wide, not local, in character. They were evident well before either the Lukouchiao incident of 1937 or the Manchurian incident of 1931.

Obviously, then, expansion on the continent was not the primary cause of economic control. War conditions have merely hastened and modulated trends without either initiating or drastically redirecting them. The failure of party cabinets was also an effect rather than a cause, for many of the major steps in economic control were taken in the period of strongest party rule.

No attempt has been made in this study to analyze Japan's foreign policy, but a careful examination of strictly internal political trends gives little support to the popular explanation of "militarism" or "totalitarianism" as the cause of Japanese policies. Such charges, if they are to be sustained at all, must find justification elsewhere. On the other hand, it is quite probable that the *world-wide* trend toward more comprehensive economic control, by placing a premium on the mobilization of natural resources, enhanced the importance of relations with

Manchuria and China in the eyes of Japanese leaders concerned with domestic and defense problems and so contributed to the situation out of which the present hostilities developed. If this is true, Japan's economic arguments deserve more careful examination than they have yet received.

Both the universality and the persistence of the causal factors make it probable that governmental control over economics and over the affairs of the individual will continue to increase. There is certainly no reason to expect a change earlier in Japan than in the United States. Cessation of the war in China or amelioration of the international situation would result in relaxation of some control measures, but major policies would probably be little affected. It is difficult to conceive of even a revolution reversing the trend toward economic control; on the contrary, any such upheaval would certainly result, at least temporarily, in a further curtailment of individual freedom of speech and action.

What guidance may these conclusions offer in a consideration of the problem of an eventual peace settlement in the Far East? In the first place, no thinking in regard to a settlement which would include Japan is likely to be sound unless it is based on the assumption that the present Japanese Government is the legitimate and accepted government of the Japanese people, and that in ability, patriotism, and social vision its leaders are neither far above nor far below the statesmen of other nations interested in the Pacific. This standard leaves, of course, ample room for the explanation of costly mistakes without recourse to an assumption that the Japanese Government and its leaders are abnormal. Secondly, the peculiar obstacles in Japan's internal organization to peace negotiations or economic agreements with any power are amply paralleled in other countries and should, therefore, be easily understood by those with a will to do so. Finally, no negotiations, either political or economic, can safely ignore the obvious determination of the Japanese Government and people to plan and direct their economic affairs. *Laissez faire* premises are likely to prove of questionable value for the constructive analysis of the problems of either a bilateral or a multilateral peace in the Pacific.

BIBLIOGRAPHICAL NOTE

Works mentioned here, but not specifically referred to within the body of the book, are marked by an asterisk*. English translations of Japanese titles are given only on first citation.

A study of contemporary Japanese political trends presents quite a different bibliographical problem than does a study of some period or process which a few decades have already safely embalmed in history. Our subject evolves and new sources appear even as we write. Western libraries are weak in Japanese materials, even in bibliographical aids; Japan is distant; mails are slow; the international book trade between Japan and the United States or Europe is yet in its infancy. Even had one unlimited funds for book purchases and unlimited time to search for new publications there would still be a lapse of some months between the publication of a new study of note in Japan and its appearance on the desk of the Western student for examination. Many of the periodicals or monographs which would have been useful were not available in the locality of the author; others were available only in broken or partial files; still others on which the author hoped to rely when this study was initiated became available only after the manuscript had been written. Some of the works desired might have been found in other libraries in the United States, but time was not available to search for them. Both the bibliography actually used in the preparation of the monograph and the more extensive list given here must, therefore, remain incomplete.

The standard sources for Japanese legislation are the *Kampo* (Official Gazette), in which all laws, ordinances, treaties, orders, appointments, regulations, etc., with the exception of a few matters of military or diplomatic secrecy, must be promulgated and the *Genko Horei Shuran** (Collection of Laws and Ordinances in Force), in which such legislation is logically classified for easy reference. The *Kampo* also includes in its extras (*Kampo Gogai*) the minutes of the sessions of the two houses of the Japanese Diet. Official reports, compilations, and periodical publications are too numerous to mention. They are catalogued in the *Kancho Kanko Tosho Geppo** (Monthly Report of Government Documents), which now runs to over one hundred pages an issue. None of these throws much light on political maneuvers. The *Shu-ho* (Weekly Bulletin), which has been published since 1937 by the Information Bureau of the Cabinet does, however, provide some comment on legislation and current government policies. The English monthly, the *Tokyo Gazette,* is an abridged and translated version of the

Shu-ho and like it provides official information and interpretations.

For trends of political controversy one must consult Japan's newspapers and magazines. Of the former there are some seven thousand in Japan but the most important are the *Osaka Mainichi** and the *Osaka Asahi** and their smaller affiliates the *Tokyo Nichi Nichi** and *Tokyo Asahi*. All four of these are now also published in monthly reduced size facsimile editions for library and reference use. These *shukusatsuhan* are complete and exact duplicates of the regular daily editions but in smaller size, on better paper, and bound. As both the *Asahi* and the *Mainichi* are moderate it is sometimes useful to consult more extreme but less influential papers such as the Tokyo *Kokumin** (Nation). However, since the various *shukusatsuhan* are provided with monthly indices they are incomparably the most useful newspaper sources. Availability of a complete file of this edition of the *Tokyo Asahi* accounts for the many references to that paper in this study. The *Asahi*, like the *New York Times*, prints full or abridged texts of many important documents.

There are four English dailies of some importance. The *Japan Times and Mail** (Tokyo) and the *Osaka Mainichi and Tokyo Nichi Nichi** are Japanese edited, the *Japan Chronicle** (Kobe) is British, and the *Japan Advertiser** (Tokyo) is American. The *Advertiser* is perhaps the most useful because of its policy of printing translations from the Japanese press, but the *Chronicle* has usually been more critical. The *Times, Chronicle,* and *Advertiser* each publish a weekly edition, and these are popular abroad as they include most of the important news of the week in compact form. The *Trans-Pacific*, which has been used for this study, is the weekly publication of the *Japan Advertiser*. These English language papers are convenient but are less complete than the *Asahi*. The foreigner depending on them for his knowledge of contemporary Japan must allow for the peculiar bias of the foreign communities of the Japanese ports which look on Japanese politics with a mixture of condescension, amusement, and indignation.

In Japan as in America no survey of current opinion on political questions is possible without consultation of a considerable number of magazines of opinion and scholarship. Let no one assume that the process is simpler on one side of the Pacific than on the other. The valuable monthly index of periodical articles in the social sciences which is published in the *Kokumin Keizai Zasshi** (Journal of Political Economy and Commercial Science) covers materials in about four hundred different Japanese publications. Obviously only a few of these are available in Europe or the United States. Among the most important journals of opinion are *Chuo Koron* (Central Review) and *Kaizo* (Reconstruction). These are in some ways similar to *Harper's* or the *Atlantic* in the United States but are more voluminous—about five hundred pages per monthly issue—and contain a much larger proportion of articles on economics, politics, or diplomacy by competent specialists. *Gaiko Jiho* (Revue Diplomatique), the leading journal on foreign relations, also publishes some current articles on questions of internal policies. *Contemporary Japan* is somewhat less representative because edited for foreigners, but its monthly time-table of significant events is very convenient.

Among more specialized publications the *Shakai Seisaku Jiho** (Social Policy Review) is particularly strong on questions of governmental control. The *Kokka Gakkai Zasshi* (The Journal of the Association of Political and Social Science) is the leading political science review, but a considerable proportion of its pages are given over to European and American rather than Japanese subjects. *Keizai Ronso** (The Economic Review) and the *Kokumin Keizai Zasshi* are important for discussions of economic questions. Some of the articles in the *Keizai Ronso* are translated in the *Kyoto University Economic Review*. The *Toyo Keizai Shimpo** and its English counterpart, *The Oriental Economist,* are indispensable for economic statistics and for their frank comments on current developments. *Toa* (East Asia) and the *Mantetsu Chosa Geppo* (South Manchuria Railway Research Monthly) provide many of the best research studies on continental policies and conditions. They should be consulted by anyone interested in Manchukuo. Those seeking further periodicals in this field should consult the indices in *Toa*, the *Mantetsu Chosa Geppo,* and the *Kokumin Keizai Zasshi* and the "Bibliographie des Principales Publications Editées dans l'Empire Japonais,"* published in the *Bulletin de la Maison Franco-Japonaise.**

These same bibliographies list many of the new books dealing with economics or politics. In normal years Japanese presses issue over twenty thousand new titles, twice the output of the United States, and economics is always one of the leading classifications. It goes without saying that the interested student will find discussions of greater or lesser value on almost any detail of the topics discussed in this study. The Japanese titles listed below are at best a rather haphazard selection of items which have come to the author's attention and which he has found useful. Among works in Western languages only those have been included which are referred to in this study, or which are of special interest in connection with developments of the last decade, or which analyse the structure of constitutional government.

PERIODICALS

Chuo Koron (Central Review). Monthly. Tokyo.
Contemporary Japan. Monthly. Tokyo. 1932+.
* *Contemporary Manchuria.* Quarterly. Dairen. 1937+.
* *The Far Eastern Review.* Monthly. Shanghai. 1904+.
Gaiko Jiho (Revue Diplomatique). Semi-monthly. Tokyo. 1898+.
* *The Japan Chronicle Weekly.* Weekly publication of the *Japan Chronicle.* Kobe.
* *Japan Times Weekly.* Weekly publication of the *Japan Times and Mail.* Tokyo 1938+. Formerly *Japan Times and Mail Overseas Weekly Edition.*
* *Journal of the Osaka University of Commerce.* Annual. Osaka. 1933+.
Kaizo (Reconstruction). Monthly. Tokyo. 1919+.
Kampo (Official Gazette). Irregular, several times a week. Tokyo. 1885+.
* *Kancho Kanko Tosho Geppo* (Monthly Report of Government Documents). Tokyo. 1938+. Formerly *Kancho Kanko Tosho Mokuroku* (Catalog of Government Documents). Quarterly. Tokyo. 1927+.
* *Keizai Ronso* (The Economic Review). Monthly. Kyoto. 1915+.
* *Keizaigaku Ronshu* (Collection of Articles on Economics). Monthly. Tokyo. 1923+.
Kokka Gakkai Zasshi (The Journal of the Association of Political and Social Science). Monthly. Tokyo. 1887+.
* *Kokumin* (Nation). Daily. Tokyo. 1890+.
* *Kokumin Keizai Zasshi* (Journal of Political Economy and Commercial Science). Monthly. Kobe. 1906+ .
Kyoto University Economic Review. Quarterly. Kyoto. 1926+.
* *Manchoukuo Chengfu Kungpao* (Manchukuo Government Gazette). Irregular, several times per week. Hsinking. 1932+.
The Manchuria Daily News. Dairen. 1908+.
Mantetsu Chosa Geppo (South Manchuria Railway Research Monthly). Dairen. 1912+.
Oriental Economist. Monthly. Tokyo. 1934+.
* *Osaka Asahi* (Osaka Morning Sun). Twice daily. Osaka. 1879+.
* *Osaka Mainichi* (Osaka Daily). Twice daily. Osaka. 1888+.
* *Osaka Mainichi and Tokyo Nichi Nichi.* English language daily. Osaka and Tokyo. 1922+.
* *Shakai Seisaku Jiho* (Social Policy Review). Monthly. Tokyo. 1920+.

Shu-ho (Weekly Bulletin). Published by the Information Bureau of the Cabinet. Tokyo. 1936+.

Toa (East Asia). Monthly. Tokyo. 1928+.

Tokyo Asahi (Tokyo Morning Sun). Twice daily. Tokyo. 1888+. The *shukusatsuhan*, or reduced size facsimile edition, on which citations in this study are based, has been published monthly since 1919.

Tokyo Gazette. Monthly. Tokyo. 1937+.

* *Tokyo Nichi Nichi* (Tokyo Day by Day). Twice daily. Tokyo. 1872+.

* *Toyo Keizai Shimpo* (Oriental Economist). Weekly. Tokyo. 1895+.

Trans-Pacific. Weekly edition of the Japan Advertiser. Tokyo. 1920+.

BOOKS AND ARTICLES

* ALLEN, G. C. *Japan the Hungry Guest.* London. 1938.

———. *Japanese Industry: its Recent Development and Present Condition.* I.P.R. Inquiry Series. New York. 1940.

ASAHI, ISOSHI. *The Economic Strength of Japan.* Tokyo. 1939.

BARNES, KATHLEEN. "Japanese Government Given Blank Check." *Far Eastern Survey.* VII. 7. April 6, 1938. pp. 79-81.

"Bibliographie des Principales Publications Editées dans l'Empire Japonais." *Bulletin de la Maison Franco-Japonaise* (Tokyo). Vol. III, Nos. 3-4, 1931. Supplements 1, 2, 3. 1932. 1933. 1934.

BLOCH, KURT. "Coal and Power Shortage in Japan." *Far Eastern Survey.* IX. 4. Feb. 14, 1940. pp. 39-45.

———. "German-Japanese Partnership in Eastern Asia." *Far Eastern Survey.* VII. 21. Oct. 26, 1938. pp. 241-245.

———. "Inflation and Prices in the Yen Bloc." *Far Eastern Survey.* VIII. 16. Aug. 2, 1939. pp. 183-190.

———. "Yen-Bloc Food Supplies Under Strain." *Far Eastern Survey.* VIII. 21. Oct. 25, 1939. pp. 250-251.

BOODY, ELIZABETH. "Manchoukuo, the Key to Japan's Foreign Exchange Problem." *Far Eastern Survey.* VI. 10. May 12, 1937. pp. 107-112.

———. "Politics and the Yen." *Far Eastern Survey.* VI. 11. May 26, 1937. pp. 117-122.

BORTON, HUGH. *Political and Social Developments in Japan since 1931, as Affecting External Relations.* I.P.R. Inquiry Series. Preliminary mimeographed edition. New York. 1939.

* CHAMBERLIN, WILLIAM HENRY. *Japan Over Asia.* Boston. 1937.

COLEGROVE, KENNETH W. "The Japanese Cabinet." *American Political Science Review.* XXX. 5. Oct., 1936. pp. 903-923.

* ———. "The Japanese Emperor." *American Political Science Review*. Vol. XXVI. Aug. and Oct. 1932. pp. 642-659, 828-845.

———. "The Japanese Privy Council." *American Political Science Review*. Vol. XXV. Aug. and Nov. 1931. pp. 589-614, 881-905.

* ———. *Militarism in Japan*. "World Affairs Books" No. 16. Boston. 1936.

* ———. "Powers and Functions of the Japanese Diet." *American Political Science Review*. Vol. XXVII and XXVIII. Dec., 1933 and Feb., 1934. pp. 885-898, 23-39.

ELCHIBEGOFF, IVAN. "More Blows at America's Transpacific Timber Trade." *Far Eastern Survey*. VIII. 18. Aug. 30, 1939. pp. 215-217.

FARLEY, MIRIAM S. "Dutch-Japanese Negotiations Resumed." *Far Eastern Survey*. IV. 16. Aug. 14, 1935. pp. 129-130.

———. "The Impact of War on Japan's Foreign Trade." *Far Eastern Survey*. VIII. 11. May 24, 1939. pp. 123-128.

———. "Japanese Army Wins Fight to Limit Dividends." *Far Eastern Survey*. VIII. 13. June 21, 1939. pp. 153-154.

———. "The National Mobilization Controversy in Japan." *Far Eastern Survey*. VIII. 3. Feb. 1, 1939. pp. 25-30.

———. *The Problem of Japanese Trade Expansion in the Postwar Situation*. I.P.R. Inquiry Series. New York. 1940.

Fifty Years of New Japan. See Okuma, Count Shigenobu. ed.

* FUJII, SHINICHI. *The Essentials of Japanese Constitutional Law*. Tokyo. 1940.

* *Genko Horei Shuran* (Compilation of Laws and Ordinances in Force). 13 loose-leaf volumes with periodical supplements. Tokyo. 1930+.

GOTO, KIYOSHI. "Taishoku Tsumitatekin oyobi Taishoku Teate Ho" (Withdrawal from Employment Reserves and Allowance Law). *Kokka Gakkai Zasshi*. L. 8. Aug. 1936. pp. 1008-1027.

GOTO, SHIMPEI. "The Administration of Formosa." *Fifty Years of New Japan*. Vol. II. pp. 530-553.

HIDAKA, MINOO. *Gunki Hogo Ho* (The Military Secrets Protection Law). Tokyo. 1937.

* HIJIKATA, SHIGEMI. *Nippon Keizai Seisaku* (Japan's Economic Policy). Tokyo. 1937.

HONJO, EIJIRO. *The Social and Economic History of Japan*. Tokyo. 1935.

Horitsugaku Jiten. See Tanaka, Sekitaro and Sueharu, Gantaro. eds.

* HUBBARD, G. E. *Eastern Industrialization and Its Effect on the West*. Rev. ed. London and New York. 1938.

INABA, SHIRO. "Nichi-Man Shikin Tosei no Senji-teki Hoko"

(Wartime Trends in Japan-Manchukuo Capital Control). *Mantetsu Chosa Geppo.* XIX. 4. April, 1939. pp. 1-33.

International Labour Office. *Industrial Labour in Japan.* Geneva. 1933.

* Ito, Marquis Hirobumi. *Commentaries on the Constitution of the Empire of Japan.* Translated by Baron Miyoji Ito. 2nd ed. Tokyo. 1906.

Iwakura, Prince T. "Senji Keizai ni okeru Waga Kaiun Seisaku" (Our Shipping Policy in War-time Economics). *Taiheiyo* (Pacific Ocean). III. 1. Jan., 1940.

* Iwasaki, Uichi. *The Working Forces in Japanese Politics. A Brief Account of Political Conflicts 1867-1920.* "Columbia University Studies in History, Economics and Public Law." New York. 1921.

Japan. Cabinet Statistical Bureau. *Dai Nippon Teikoku Tokei Nenkan* (Statistical Yearbook of the Japanese Empire).

Japan. Department of Education. *Kokutai no Hongi* (The True Meaning of the National Polity). Tokyo. 1937.

The Japan Year Book. Annual publication of the Foreign Affairs Association of Japan. Tokyo. 1933+.

Japan-Manchoukuo Year Book. Annual. Tokyo. 1933 (1934 edition)+.

* Kaempf, Christoph. *Der Wandel im japanischen Staatsdenken der Gegenwart unter besonderer Berücksichtigung der Stellung des Tenno.* "Abhandlungen des Instituts für Politik, ausländisches öffentliches Recht und Völkerrecht an der Universität Leipzig." Leipzig. 1938.

* Kawada, Tetsuji. *Nippon Kokka Shugi no Hatten.* (Development of Statism in Japan). Tokyo. 1938.

* Kazahaya, Yasoji. *Nippon Shakai Seisaku Shi.* (History of Japanese Social Policy). Tokyo. 1937.

Keizaigaku Jiten. See Osaka Shoka Daigaku.

Kimpara, Kennosuke. "Boeki-sho Ron" (On a Department of Trade). *Kaizo.* XXI. 12. Nov., 1939. pp. 65-71.

* Kimura, Magohachiro. *Japan's Agrarian Problems.* Tokyo. 1937.

* Kojima, Seiichi. *Senji Nippon Jukogyo* (Japanese Heavy Industry in War Time). Tokyo. 1938.

* Matsui, Haruo. *Keizai Sambo Hombu Ron* (Argument for an Economic General Staff). Tokyo. 1934.

Matsukata, Kojiro. "Tosei Ichigen-ka no Kyumu" (The Urgency of Unification of Control). *Chuo Koron.* LIV. 5. May, 1939. pp. 352-353.

* Maurette, Fernand. *Social Aspects of Industrial Development in Japan.* Geneva. 1934.

* Mitsubishi Economic Research Bureau. *Japanese Trade and Industry, Present and Future.* London, 1936.
MIYAZAWA, TOSHIYOSHI. "Gyosei Kiko" (Administrative Machinery). *Kokka Gakkai Zasshi.* LIII. 9. Sept., 1939. pp. 1196-1227.
MORIGUCHI, SHIGEHARU. "Academic Freedom and the Takikawa Case." *Kaizo.* July, 1933. Translated in *Contemporary Japan.* II. 2. Sept., 1933. pp. 327-330.
NAGAOKA, RYUICHIRO. "Kanryo no Konjaku." (Bureaucracy Past and Present). *Chuo Koron.* LIV. 3. March, 1939. pp. 151-159.
NAKANO, TOMIO. "Kempo to Seiji no Kyoka" (The Constitution and the Strengthening of Politics). *Chuo Koron.* LIV. 8. Aug., 1939. pp. 4-19.
* ———. *The Ordinance Power of the Japanese Emperor.* "Johns Hopkins University Studies in Historical and Political Science." Extra volumes. New Series, No. 2. Baltimore. 1923.
NASU, SHIROSHI. "Ziele und Ausrichtung der japanischen Agrarpolitik in der Gegenwart." *Weltwirtschaftliches Archiv.* XLVI. 1. July, 1937. pp. 157-182.
NORMAN, E. HERBERT. *Japan's Emergence as a Modern State.* I.P.R. Inquiry Series. New York. 1940.
ODELL, H. "Efforts to Stimulate Domestic Airplane Output in Japan." *Far Eastern Survey.* IX. 3. Jan. 31, 1940. pp. 37-38.
OGATA, SHO. "Koa-in no Shuppatsu" (The Start of the China Board). *Kaizo,* XXI. 1. Jan., 1939. pp. 113-117.
OKUMA, COUNT SHIGENOBU. ed. *Fifty Years of New Japan.* English version edited by Marcus B. Huish. 2 vols. 2nd ed. London. 1910.
* OMURA, BUNJI. *The Last Genro. Prince Saionji, the Man Who Westernized Japan.* Philadelphia. 1938.
Osaka Shoka Daigaku. Keizai Kenkyujo. *Keizaigaku Jiten.* (Dictionary of Economics). 7 vols. Tokyo. 1930-1936.
* PFLEIDERER, OTTO. *Pfund, Yen und Dollar in der Weltwirtschaftskrise.* Berlin. 1937.
* QUIGLEY, HAROLD S. *Japanese Government and Politics.* New York. 1932.
* REISCHAUER, ROBERT KARL. *Japan, Government-Politics.* New York. 1939.
ROYAMA, MASAMICHI. "Die Wirtschaftsrechtliche Struktur als Grundlage des Japanischen Wirtschaftsaufschwungs." *Weltwirtschaftliches Archiv.* XLVI. 1. July, 1937. pp. 78-92.
SASA, HIROO. "Kokumin Soshiki Mondai no Kento" (Study of the Problem of National Organization). *Chuo Koron.* LIV. 1. Jan., 1939. pp. 30-40.

SATO, SHOSUKE. "Hokkaido and its Progress in Fifty Years." *Fifty Years of New Japan*. Vol. II. pp. 513-529.

SATOMI, IWAO. "Ikkoku Itto no Kokutaigaku-teki Hihan." (Criticism of the Principle of a Single Party from the Point of View of the Study of the National Polity). *Chuo Koron*. LIV. 1. Jan., 1939. pp. 76-84.

SEBALD, W. J. *A Selection of Japan's Emergency Legislation*. Kobe. 1937.

SHIMIZU, CHO. "Kanri Seido no Kaisei ni Kansuru Kanken" (Views on the Reform of the Civil Service System). *Kokka Gakkai Zasshi*. LI. 8. pp. 1025-1039.

SHIOMI, SABURO. "The Incidence of Taxation upon the Rural Population under War Conditions." *Kyoto University Economic Review*. XIV. 2. April, 1939. pp. 24-32.

* STEIN, GUENTHER. *Made in Japan*. London. 1935.

STEWART, JOHN R. "Japan Still Seeks Oil from Coal and Shale." *Far Eastern Survey*. VIII. 2. Jan. 19, 1939. pp. 22-23.

SUGIYAMA, HEISUKE. "Sodoin Ho Dai Shi Jo no Hatsudo" (Invocation of Art. 4 of the General Mobilization Law). *Kaizo*. XXI. 5. May, 1939. pp. 214-222.

TAKAHASHI, KAMEKICHI. *Nippon Keizai Tosei Ron* (Japanese Economic Control). Tokyo. 1933.

* ———. *Senji Keizai no Gendankai to sono Zento* (Present Stage of War Time Economy and Its Future). Tokyo. 1938.

* ———. *Senso to Nippon Keizai Ryoku* (War and Japan's Economic Strength). Tokyo. 1937.

TAKEKOSHI, YOSABURO. *The Economic Aspects of the History of the Civilization of Japan*. 3 vols. New York and London. 1930.

* TAKEUCHI, STERLING TATSUJI. *War and Diplomacy in the Japanese Empire*. New York. 1935.

TANAKA, JIRO. "Fuon Bunsho Rinji Torishimari Ho ni Tsuite" (Regarding the Emergency Seditious Literature Control Law). *Kokka Gakkai Zasshi*. L. 8. Aug., 1936. pp. 1028-1040.

TANAKA, SEKITARO AND SUEHARU, GANTARO. eds. *Horitsugaku Jiten* (Dictionary of Jurisprudence). Tokyo. 1934-1937.

TANIGUCHI, KICHIHIKO. *Boeki Tosei Ron* (Trade Control). Tokyo. 1934.

———. "The Development of the Link System in Japan." *Kyoto University Economic Review*. XIV. 3. pp. 1-22.

———. "The Link System in Japan." *Kyoto University Economic Review*. XIV. 2. April, 1939. pp. 33-54.

* ———. *Nippon Boeki Seisaku* (Japan's Trade Policy). Tokyo. 1937.

* TANIN, O., AND YOHAN, E. *Militarism and Fascism in Japan.* New York and London. 1934.
* ———. *When Japan Goes to War.* New York. 1936.
* Tokyo Nichi Nichi Shimbun. *Senji Keizai no Jissai Mondai* (Practical Problems of War Time Economy). Tokyo. 1938.

URABE, HYAKUTARO. "Ika ni Naikaku Seido wo Kyoka Seshimubeki Ya" (How Should We Strengthen the Cabinet System). *Gaiko Jiho.* LXXXIX. 1. Jan. 1, 1939. pp. 85-100.
* UYEDA, TEIJIRO. *The Recent Development of Japanese Foreign Trade.* Tokyo. 1936.
* ———. *The Small Industries of Japan. Their Growth and Development.* London and Shanghai. 1938.

VAKIL, C. N. AND D. N. MALUSTE. *Commercial Relations between India and Japan.* "Studies in Indian Economics." Calcutta. 1937.
* WASHIO, YOSHINAO. ed. *Inukai Bokudo Den* (Biography of Inukai Ki). 3 vols. Tokyo. 1938-1939.

YABE, TADAHARU. "Gikai Seido" (The Diet System). *Kokka Gakkai Zasshi.* LIII. 9. Sept., 1939. pp. 1161-1194.

YASUO, NAGAHARU. "Manchukuo's New Economic Policy." *Pacific Affairs.* XI. 3. Sept., 1938. pp. 323-337.

———. "The North Ocean Fishery in Japan's Economic Life." *Far Eastern Survey.* VIII. 9. April 26, 1939. pp. 106-108.
* YOUNG, A. MORGAN. *Imperial Japan, 1926-1938.* New York and London. 1938.

INDEX

Abe Cabinet, 68, 73 n.
Academic freedom, 82
Adachi, advocacy coalition cabinet, 67, 75
Administrative reorganization, 62-71
Advisory organs, 63-66
Africa, control exports to, 13
Agricultural security, 24, 29-37
Agriculture and Forestry, Dept. of, 23, 33, 70, 71
Aizawa, assassin, 84
Alcohol, 47
Allen, G. C., 11 n.
Aluminum, 49
Ammonium sulphate, 13, 34-35
Anshan, 39, 47
Anti-Comintern Pact, 16 n.
Aoki Ichio, 17 n.
Army, censorship by, 86
  and economic control, 40, 48-49
  internal control, 78-79
  political role, 66-68, 71-72, 77-80
  See also Kwantung Army
Asahi Isoshi, 22 n.
Assassinations, 73, 78, 84
Assimilation, in colonial policies, 44
Associated Press (U. S.), 85
Australia, trade dispute and agreement with, 15-16, 21, 41
Automotive industry, 46
Autonomous Shipping Control Commission, 21
Aviation, 48

Baba, Minister of Finance, 65
Bank of Agriculture and Industry, 36
Bank of Chosen, 41
Bank of Japan, 18, 20, 41, 59
Bank of Taiwan, 10
Barnes, Kathleen, 50 n.
Beet sugar, 37
Beikoku Tosei Iinkai: See Rice Control Commission
Belshaw, H., 32
Bilateral trade agreements, 14-17
Bloch, Kurt, 16 n., 28 n., 43 n.
Bocki Shingi-kai: See Trade Council
Bonds, government, 58-59
Boody, Elizabeth, 18
Brazil, "link" for exports to, 20 n.

Breweries, 37
Bristles, 20
British Broadcasting Company, 85
British North Borneo, control exports to, 13
Budget, 57-58, 76
Bulletin de la Maison Franco-Japonaise, 92
Bureau of Mines (U. S.), 45 n.
Burma, trade agreement with, 15

Cabinet (Great Britain), 69
Cabinet, political structure of, 67-70
  and Diet, 71-80
  appointment, 81
  new agencies under, 70
Cabinet Information Bureau, 85
Cabinet Inquiry Bureau, 64, 65, 68
Cabinet Inquiry Council, 64
Calcium Cyanamide, 34
Camphor, 37
Canada, 1935 trade dispute with, 16
Canneries, 37
Capital, control of, 17, 19, 42-43, 50-51, 59-60
  tax on, 60
Capital Issues Commission (U. S.), 59
Carbide, 25
Cement, 25
Censorship: *See* Freedom of speech
Central Bank of Manchu, 41, 42
Central Bank of the Production Cooperatives, 36
Central China Promotion Company, 38
Central Cocoon Price-Fixing Commission, 32
Central Depository for Commercial and Industrial Guilds, 27
Central Economic Conference, 65
Central League for Election Purification, 83
Central Review (Japanese periodical), 92
Ceramics, 13, 15
Chemical industry, 49
Chiho jichi undo: See Local autonomy movement
China, and economic control in Japan, 4, 5, 38, 39, 42, 43
China Board, 66, 69, 80

101

INDEX

China Development Company, 38
Chinese affairs, proposed department of, 71
Chuo Keizai Kaigi: See Central Economic Conference.
Chuo Koron: See Central Review
Chu-Shi Shinko Kaisha: See Central China Promotion Company
Civil service, 6, 57, 67, 71-72, 77, 81
Clayton Act (U. S.), 5
Coal, 37, 39
Coal Mining Act (Great Britain), 25
Coalition cabinet, advocacy of, 67, 72
Co-education, 82
Colegrove, Kenneth W., 67 *n.*, 81 *n.*
Collection of Laws and Ordinances in Force, 90
Colonial areas, economic control in, 37-44
Commerce and Industry, Dept. of, 20, 23, 46, 47, 70, 71
Committee on Administrative Reorganization (U. S.), 77
Communications, Dept. of, 48, 70
Communism, 83
Conciliation, 35
Concordia Society (Manchukuo), 75
Conscription, incongruity with *laissez-faire*, 6
of labor, 51, 55-56
Conseil National Economique (France), 63
Consiglio Nazionale delle Corporazioni (Italy), 63
Constitution, 5-6, 66, 71, 75
Consumers, representation of, 28
Contemporary Japan, 92
Continental policy, 80, 88
Control Committee, 25
Control Consultation Board, 19
Cooperatives, 30, 33-36
 See also Guilds
Copper, 19, 25
Cotton and cotton goods, 13, 15, 17, 19-20, 25, 28, 32, 37, 38, 42, 43
Council on Commerce and Industry, 47
Crab canneries, 22
Cuba, trade negotiations with, 14

Dai Nippon Yushutsu Meriyasu Kabushiki Kaisha: See Japan Export Hosiery Company
Daladier, Premier, 66

Dan Takuma, Baron, 73, 84
"Dangerous thoughts," control of, 83
Debt, public, growth of, 58
Deficits, budgetary, 58
Delegation of powers, 6
Departments, independence, 67
 reorganization, 70-71
Dictatorship, improbability of, 68
Diet, 71-81, 90
Diet System Inquiry Commission, 76
Direct appeal to the throne, 67, 80
Discharge allowances, 55
Domei Tsushin-sha, 85
Drought relief, 54
Due-process clause, 6
Dutch East Indies, trade dispute and agreement with, 13, 15, 21

Earthquake, Tokyo, 1923, economic effects, 10
Earthquakes, relief in case of, 54
East Asia (Japanese periodical), 92
East Asia Shipping Company, 21-22
Economic Advisory Council (England), 64
Economic councils, 63
"Economic general staff," 64
Economic Review (Japanese), 92
Education, 52, 56, 81-87
Education, Dept. of, 82, 83
Elchibegoff, Ivan, 23 *n.*
Elder statesmen, 67, 78
Elections, 72-74, 83
Electric bulbs, 13, 14
Electric power, 48-49, 51, 80
Emergency cabinet councillors, 68
Emergency Capital Adjustment Commission, 59
Emergency Industrial Council, 24
Emergency Industrial Rationalization Bureau, 24
Emergency Powers Bill (Great Britain), 50
Emergency Price Policy Commission, 28
Emigration, encouragement of, 54
Emperor, attempt on life of, 73
Employment, control over, 51, 55
Employment bureaus, 55
"Ever Normal Granary," 29
Excess profits tax, 60
Exchange: *See* Foreign exchange
Exchange dumping, charges of, 13

INDEX

Executive, influence, 69, 81
   leadership by, 63
   and legislature, 71-80
   weakness, 66-68
Expenditures, military, increase in, 58
Export associations, 11-17, 26
Exports, control of, 11-20, 26, 30, 32, 60
Extraterritoriality, surrender of, 42

Family system, and unemployment, 54
Farley, Miriam S., 15 n., 19 n., 23 n., 35 n., 50 n., 51 n.
Farm problems: *See* Agricultural security
Federated American Engineering Societies, 24 n.
Federation of Pencil Exporters' Associations, 14
Fertilizer industry, control of, 33-35, 49
Fertilizer Investigation Commission, 34
Finance, 57-61
Finance, Dept. of, 20, 70
Fires, relief in case of, 54
Fisher, Galen M., 33 n.
Fishing, 20, 22, 29, 54
Five-minister conference, 69
Five-Year Plan (Manchukuo), 41, 42, 46
Floods, relief in case of, 54
Flour, 25, 37
Food, near self-sufficiency in, 28
Foreign Affairs, Dept. of, 70, 77, 83, 86
Foreign Currency Valuation Commission, 18
Foreign exchange, control of, 17-20, 40-42, 59
Foreign Exchange Control Commission, 18
Foreign trade, legislation, 16, 17, 18, 30
   policy, 9-24
   proposed dept. of, 70
   vulnerability to control, 7
Formosa, 29, 37-39, 43
France, comparisons to, 5, 44, 50, 53, 63, 66, 83 n., 85-88
   influence on Japan, 3
Freedom of speech, 81-87
Fuels Investigation Commission, 47
Fushun, 39

Gaika Hyoka Iinkai: See Foreign Currency Valuation Commission
Gaiko Jiho: See Revue Diplomatique

Gaikoku Kawase Kanri Iinkai: See Foreign Exchange Control Commission
General Mobilization Commission, 51, 52
General Mobilization Law, 32, 42, 50-53, 55, 56, 62, 68, 69, 80
Generals, as premiers, 73
Genko Horei Shuran: See Collection of Laws and Ordinances in Force
Genro: See Elder statesmen
Germany, comparisons to, 24, 25, 44, 63, 75, 85, 87
   influence on Japan, 3
   trade agreements, 16, 41
   World War experience, 7, 8
Gesetz über Errichtung von Zwangskartellen (Germany), 25
Giin-ho: See Law of the Houses
Gold, 11, 37, 59
Gosplan (U. S. S. R.), 63
Goto Kiyoshi, 55 n.
Goto Shimpei, on monopolies, 38
Government publications, catalog, 90
   increase, 83
Grants in aid, local, 58, 60, 82
Great Britain, colonial policies, 15
   comparisons to, 3, 5, 6, 17, 25, 44, 47, 50, 53, 56, 63, 66, 69, 77, 85, 86, 87, 88
   devaluation of pound, 10
   oil companies, 47
Guilds, 4, 11, 12, 26, 27, 33, 35

Hamaguchi Yuko, Premier, 24, 27, 84
Handicraft industries, 5
Havas (French), 85
Hayashi Cabinet, 65, 73, 75, 76
Hayashi Senjuro, Minister of Army, 78
Health insurance, 56-57
Hidaka Minoo, 87 n.
Hiranuma Cabinet, 68, 75, 77
Hirota Cabinet, 49, 65, 86
Hiryo Chosa Iinkai: See Fertilizer Investigation Commission
Hito-no-michi, suppression of, 84
Hokkaido, 37, 38
Hokkaido Development Administration, 37
Hokkaido Kaitakushi: See Hokkaido Development Administration
Hoku-Shi Kaihatsu Kaisha: See North China Development Company
Holland, influence on Japan, 3

Holmes, Justice, 88
Home Affairs, Dept. of, 70, 72, 84, 86
Honjo Eijiro, 4 *n.*
Hoover, Herbert, President, 24 *n.*, 50 *n.*, 63
Hoshino Naoki, 42
Hosiery, 22
House of Peers, 50, 66, 72, 75-76, 80, 81
House of Representatives, 50, 66, 80
Housing, 56
Hsing Chung Kung-Ssu: See China Development Company
Hypothec Bank, 27

Ice, 26
Ikeda Seihin, 28, 60
Ikeda Torajiro, 35 *n.*
Ikki Kitokuro, 82
Imperial Fuel Industry Company, 47
Imperial Silk Company, 31, 32
Imperial universities, 82
"Imperial Way," 54
Imports, control of, 18-20
  See also Foreign trade
Inaba Shiro, 43 *n.*
India, trade agreement with, 15
Industrial Bank, 27, 36
Industrial Bank of Manchukuo, 41
Industrial Control Bureau, 24 *n.*
Industrial Efficiency Act (New Zealand), 25
Industrial recovery, 24-29
Information, trends in govt. policy, 81-87
Ino Sekiya, 30 *n.*
Inoue Junnosuke, assassination of, 73, 84
Inquiry Bureau: *See* Cabinet Inquiry Bureau
Insurance, 36, 54, 56, 57
International Labour Office, 55
Inukai Ki, Premier, assassination of, 73, 84
Inukai Cabinet, 27
Iron and steel, 19, 28, 39, 42, 45-46
Iron and Steel Control Council, 45
Iron and Steel Industry Act (New Zealand), 45 *n.*
Italy, comparisons to, 63, 75, 87
  trade agreement with, 16
Iwakura, Prince T., 20 *n.*, 21 *n.*
Iwasaki Hiroshi, 35 *n.*

Japan Advertiser, 91
Japan-American Lumber Imports Company, 22-23
Japan Ammonium Sulphate Company, 34
Japan Aviation Company, 48
Japan Broadcasting Association, 85
Japan Central Silk Association, 31
Japan Chronicle, 91
Japan Export Hosiery Company, 22
Japan Export Umbrella Company, 22 *n.*
Japan Gold Production Encouragement Corporation, 59
Japan Iron Manufacturing Company, 45-46
Japan Knitted Goods Export Guild, 13
Japan - Manchukuo - China Economic Council, 43
Japan-Manchukuo economic bloc, 39-44
Japan-Manchukuo Economic Commission, 40
Japan-Manchukuo Iron and Steel Sales Company, 46
Japan Marine Products Sales Company, 23
Japan Rice Company, 30
Japan Sea Marine Transportation Company, 21
Japan to Africa and Near East Export Guild, 14
Japan to India Cotton Goods Export Association, 15
Japan-Russia Fishery Company, 22
Japan Times and Mail, 91
Java, 15
Jidosha Kogyo Kabushiki Kaisha: See Motor Car Industrial Company
Journal of the Association of Political and Social Science (Japanese), 92
Journal of Political Economy and Commercial Science, 91, 92
Judicial review, absence of, 6
Jushin: See Ministers close to the throne
Justice, Dept. of, 84
Juyo Sangyo Tosei Ho: See Major Industries Control Law

Kabunakama, 4
Kaizo: See Reconstruction
Kampo: See Official Gazette
Kancho Kanko Tosho Geppo: See Monthly Report of Government Documents

INDEX

Kan-in, Prince, Chief of Staff, 78
Karafuto, 29, 39, 43
Kartell Gesetz (Germany), 25
Kato Taka-akira, Premier, 12
Keizai Ronso: See Economic Review
Keizai sambo hombu: See "Economic general staff"
Kenkyu-kai, 76
Kikaku-cho: See Planning Office
Kikaku-in: See Planning Board
Kimpara Kennosuke, 17 n., 70 n.
Kishi Shinsuke, 11 n., 25 n., 34 n.
Kita Ikki, execution of, 84
Kiyasu Kenjiro, 46 n.
Koa-in: See China Board
Kodo: See "Imperial Way"
Kogyo Ginko: See Industrial Bank
Kokka Gakkai Zasshi: See Journal of the Association of Political and Social Science
Kokka Sodoin Shingi-kai: See General Mobilization Commission
Kokumin: See The Nation
Kokumin Keizai Zasshi: See Journal of Political Economy and Commercial Science
Kokumin seikatsu antei: See "Stabilization of the national livelihood"
Konoe, Fumimaro, Prince, 68, 75-77
Konoe Cabinet, 68, 75, 77
Korea, 29, 37-39, 43
Koro Tosei Iinkai: See Navigation Routes Control Commission
Kosei-sho: See Public Welfare, Dept. of
Kumiai: See Guilds
Kusumi Issei, 36 n., 56 n.
Kwantung Army, 39-40, 41, 80
Kwantung Bureau, 40, 41
Kwantung Leased Territory, 40, 42, 43, 80
Kyoto Imperial University, 82
Kyoto University Economic Review, 92
Kyowa-kai: See Concordia Society

Labor, disputes, 55
  legislation, 35 n., 51, 52, 55-56
  proposed department of, 71
Labor Government (England), 64
Law of the Houses, 76
Leadership: *See* political leadership
League of Nations, 39
Leather, 28
Legislation, compilations of, 90
Legislative Bureau, 65

Legislature, 63, 71-81
"Link" system, 19-20
Lloyd George, David, 69 n.
Local autonomy movement, 83
London Naval Treaty, 72, 78
Lorwin, Lewis L., 64
Lukouchiao Incident, effect, 58
Lumber, 22-23, 37

MacDonald, Ramsay, 64
Machine tools, 53
Magazines, 91, 92
Magnesium, 49
Major Industries Control Law, 1931, 25, 27, 28, 45, 46
Maluste, D. N., 15 n.
Manchukuo: *See* Manchuria and Manchukuo
Manchuria and Manchukuo, 15, 16, 37-44, 47, 92
Manchuria Heavy Industrial Development Company, 41
Manchurian Affairs Bureau, 40, 41, 65, 66, 80
Manchurian incident, effect, 58, 72
Mandated Islands, 38-39, 43
Manhood suffrage, 74
Manila hemp, 20 n.
Manshu Jukogyo Kaihatsu Kaisha: See Manchuria Heavy Industrial Development Company
Mantetsu Chosa Geppo: See South Manchuria Railway Research Monthly
Marco Polo Bridge incident: *See* Lukouchiao incident
Marine products, 23
Matches, 13
Matsukata Kojiro, 71 n.
Matsuoka Yosuke, 40, 75
Mazaki, Inspector-General of Military Education, 78
Medical insurance: *See* Health insurance
Meiji University, 82
Metals, shortage of, 28
  non-ferrous, 46, 49
  light, 53
  See also Minerals and mining
Minami Jiro, General, 40
Minerals and mining, 53, 55
Ministers, appointment and responsibility, 67
Ministers close to the throne, 66, 72, 81

INDEX

Ministers without portfolio, 68
Minobe Tatsukichi, 82
Minorities, representation of, 74
Minseito, 64, 73, 77
   Cabinet, 10, 25, 27, 31, 67
Mitsubishi, 26
Mitsui, 26
Miyazawa Toshiyoshi, 62 n., 67 n., 69 n.
Mongolia, 38, 43
Monopolies, 5, 20-24, 27, 85
Monthly Report of Government Documents, 90
Moriguchi Shigeji, 82 n.
Motor Car Industrial Company, 46
Muscle Shoals, 9

Nagaoka Ryuichiro, 77 n.
Nagata Tetsuzan, 44, 78, 84
Nagoya Imperial University, 82
Naikaku Joho-bu: See Cabinet Information Bureau
Naikaku Shingi-kai: See Cabinet Inquiry Council.
Naikaku Shingi Kyoku: See Cabinet Inquiry Bureau
Nakano Tomio, 70 n.
Nasu Shiroshi, 33 n., 36 n.
Nation (Japanese daily), 91
National Conference on Protection of Commercial Rights, 33 n.
National defense, and economic control, 44-53
National Industrial Recovery Act (U. S.), 25, 27
National policy concerns, 21-22, 23 n., 30, 38, 48
Navigation: *See* Shipping
Navigation Routes Control Commission, 21
Navy, censorship by, 86
   and economic control, 48
   internal control, 78
   political role, 66, 67, 71-72, 77-80
Nenryo Chosa Iinkai: See Fuels Investigation Commission
New Guinea, control exports to, 13
New Zealand, comparison to, 12 n., 16 n., 19 n., 25, 32, 45 n.
Newspapers, 91
   See also Press, control of
Nichi-Ro Gyogyo Kaisha: See Japan-Russia Fishery Company
Nippon Chuo San Shi Kai: See Japan Central Silk Association

Nippon Dempo, 85
Nippon Industrial Company, 41
Nippon Kai Kaiun Kaisha: See Japan Sea Marine Transportation Company
Nippon Kozai Rengo-kai: See Nippon Steel Materials Federation
Nippon Menorimono Tai Indo Yushutsu Kumiai: See Japan to India Cotton Goods Export Association
Nippon Ryuan Kabushiki Kaisha: See Japan Ammonium Sulphate Company
Nippon Steel Materials Federation, 45-46
Nishio Suehiro, expulsion from Diet, 68
Noko Ginko: See Bank of Agriculture and Industry
Non-recognition, 39
Norman, E. H., 5 n.
North China Development Company, 38
North Korea Railways, 41
Nosangyoson Keizai Kosei Undo: See Rural reconstruction movement

Occupational representation, 75
Odell, Lawrence H., 48 n.
Official Gazette, 90
Ogata Hanshi, 15 n.
Ogata Kiyoshi, 11 n.
Ogata Sho, 66 n.
Ohara Sei, 23 n.
Oil, mineral, 28, 39, 46-48
   vegetable, 25
Okada Cabinet, 34, 64
Omotokyo, suppression of, 84
Ordinance power, 6
Oriental Development Company, 38
Oriental Economist, 92
Osaka Asahi, 91
Osaka Imperial University, 82
Osaka Mainichi, 91
Osaka Mainichi and *Tokyo Nichi Nichi,* 91
Otsuki Masao, 35 n.
Overseas Affairs, Dept. of, 39-40, 70
Oyama Iwao, elder statesman, 78

Pact for Renunciation of War, 72
Paper, 20 n., 25

INDEX

Parties, 71-81
    See also Minseito, Seiyukai, Toho-kai, Social Mass Party, Social Democratic Party
Party, advocacy single, 74-75
Patriotism, abuses of, 83-84
Pawn shops, 56
Peace Preservation Law, 72, 83, 84, 86
Pencils, 14
People's Bank, 56
Petroleum Industry Commission, 47
Philippine Islands, 14, 39, 43-44
Phosphates, 34, 38-39
Planning Board, 41, 65-66
Planning Office, 65
Political leadership, problem of, 66-70
Post office, in elections, 74
    insurance, 56
    rates, 60
    sale of bonds, 59
    savings, 43
Premier: See Executive
Press, control of, 84-87
Prices, control of, 11-14, 25-29, 31, 32, 52, 57
Primary Products Marketing Act (New Zealand), 32
Privy Council, 66, 71-72, 80
Productive equipment, control expansion of, 59
Proletarian parties, 74
    See also Toho-kai, Social Mass Party, and Social Democratic Party
Propaganda, trends in govt. policy, 81-87
Proportional representation, 74
Public opinion, 8, 63, 81-87
Public Welfare, Dept. of, 56, 57, 70, 80
Pulp, 20

Quotas, 13

Radio, 84-85
Railway General Directorate (Hsinking), 41
Railways, 5
Railways, Dept. of, 46, 48
Rationalization, 24-25
Rationing, 28, 47
Rayon, 13, 17, 20, 25
Reconstruction (Japanese periodical), 92
Referendum, 63

Reichskuratorium für Wirtschaftlichkeit (Germany), 24 *n.*
Reichswirtschaftsrat (Germany), 63
Relief, agrarian, 54, 80
    unemployment, 54
    for veterans, 55, 57
Rengo, 85
Rents, control, 35 *n.*, 52
Research, compulsory, 52
Reservists' Association, 79, 83
Resources, control of, 53
    investigation, 44-45
Resources Board, 65
Resources Bureau, 44-45, 49, 64
Resources Council, 63-64
Retaliatory tariffs, 16
Reuters (British), 85
Revue Diplomatique (Japanese periodical), 92
Rice, 29-30, 32, 39, 51
Rice Control Commission, 30
Rinji Bukka Taisaku Iinkai: See Emergency Price Policy Commission
Rinji naikaku sangi: See Emergency cabinet councillors
Rinji Sangyo Gori Kyoku: See Emergency Industrial Rationalization Bureau
Rinji Sangyo Shingi-kai: See Emergency Industrial Council
Rinji Shikin Chosei Iinkai: See Emergency Capital Adjustment Commission
Roosevelt, President Franklin D., 58 *n.*, 63, 77
Royama Masamichi, 65
Rural credit, 35
Rural reconstruction movement, 33

Saghalien: *See* Karafuto
Saionji Kimmochi, Prince, 73
Saito Cabinet, 27, 68, 69
Sakuradamon affair, 1932, 73
Sales tax, 60
Salt, 37
Sangyo Kumiai Chuo Kinko: See Central Bank of the Production Cooperatives
Sangyo Tosei Kyoku: See Industrial Control Bureau
Sasa Hiroo, 75 *n.*
Sato Shosuke, 37 *n.*
Satomi Iwao, 75 *n.*
Schools: *See* Education

INDEX

Sebald, W. J., 17 n., 19 n., 34 n., 60 n.
Securities, regulation and taxation of, 59-60
See also Bonds, government
Seditious literature: See Press, control of
Seinen gakko: See Youth schools
Seinendan: See Young Men's Associations
Seiyukai, 64, 68, 73, 77, 80 n.
Sekiyugyo Iinkai: See Petroleum Industry Commission
Senkyo Shukusei Chuo Remmei: See Central League for Election Purification
Shakai Minshu-to: See Social Democratic Party
Shakai Seisaku Jiho: See Social Policy Review
Shakai Taishu-to: See Social Mass Party
Shanghai Truce, 1932, 80
Sherman Anti-trust Act (U. S.), 4, 5
Shidehara, Min. Foreign Affairs, 27
Shigen Kyoku: See Resources Bureau
Shigen Shingi-kai: See Resources Council
Shika Antei Iinkai: See Silk Price Stabilization Commission
Shimizu Cho, 77 n.
Shiomi Saburo, 61 n.
Shipping and navigation, 15, 20-22, 49, 50, 52, 55
Shogunate: See Tokugawa shogunate
Shoko Kumiai Chuo Kinko: See Central Depository for Commercial and Industrial Guilds
Shoko Shingi-kai: See Council on Commerce and Industry
Shoko Shingi-kai Sangyo Gorika ni Kansuru Tokubetsu Iinkai: See Special Committee on Industrial Rationalization of the Council on Commerce and Industry
Shomin Kinko: See People's Bank
Shu-ho: See Weekly Bulletin
Showa Iron Works, 46
Silk, 13, 25, 29, 30-33, 54
Silk Price Stabilization Commission, 32
Silver, 59
Single party, advocacy of, 74-75
Social Democratic Party, 38
Social dumping, charges of, 13
Social Policy Review (Japanese), 92
Social Mass Party, 37, 49, 68, 75

South Manchuria Railway Company, 38-41
South Manchuria Railway Concession, 80
South Manchuria Railway Research Monthly, 92
South Manchuria Railway zone, 42
Special Committee on Industrial Rationalization of the Council on Commerce and Industry, 24
Stabilization of the national livelihood, 7, 24
Stewart, John R., 48 n.
Straits Settlements, control exports to, 13
Subsidies, reasons for, 5
to automotive industry, 46
to aviation, 48
to farming, 36
to guilds, 27
to insurance, 54
to shipping, 20-21
Subversive activities, suppression of, 83-84
Sugar, 25, 37, 38
Sugiyama Heisuke, 51 n.
Sulphuric acid, 25
Sumitomo, 26
Sutch, W. B., 16 n.
Switzerland, 3
Syria, trade agreement with, 14

Taiman Jimukyoku: See Manchurian Affairs Bureau
Taiwan: See Formosa
Takahashi Kamekichi, 11 n., 25 n., 34 n.
Takekoshi Yosaburo, 4 n.
Takikawa, Prof., expulsion of, 82
Tamaya Muneichiro, 64 n.
Tanaka Jiro, Premier, 45 n., 86 n.
Tanaka Cabinet, 34
Tangku Truce, 1933, 80
Taniguchi Kichihiko, 12 n., 13 n., 15 n., 16 n., 20 n.
Tariffs, 5, 10-11, 13-17
Taxation, 58, 60-61
Technical training, legislation re, 52
Teikoku San Shi Kabushiki Kaisha: See Imperial Silk Company
Tekko Tosei Kyogi-kai: See Iron and Steel Control Council
Telegraph, 4-5
Terauchi, Minister of Army, 79
Textiles: See Cotton and cotton goods

INDEX

Tiles, 26
Toa: See East Asia
Toa Kaiun Kabushiki Kaisha: See East Asia Shipping Company
Tobacco, 60
Toho-kai, 37, 75
Tohoku area, depression in, 54
Tokugawa shogunate, 4
Tokyo Asahi, 12 *n.*, 38, 73, 91
Tokyo Gazette, 90
Tokyo Imperial University, 82
Tokyo Nichi Nichi, 91
Tominaga Yugi, 10 *n.*
Tosei Iinkai: See Control Committee
Tosei Kyogi-kai: See Control Consultation Board
Toyama Mitsuru, 75
Toynbee, Arnold J., 73 *n.*
Toyo Keizai Shimpo, 92
Trade associations, 11-17
  See also Kumiai, Kabunakama, Guilds
Trade Council, 19
Trade unions, 55
Trans-Pacific, 91
Treasury Deposits Bureau, 27
Treaties, unequal, 5, 10
Turkey, trade agreement with, 14
Turner, B. R., 19 *n.*, 45 *n.*

Ugaki, General, 37, 79
Umbrellas, 22 *n.*, 26
Unemployment, relief for, 54
U. S. S. R., comparisons to, 63, 64, 75, 87
  example of, 7
  fisheries, 22
Union of South Africa, 15-16
United Press (U. S.), 85
United States, agreement re P. I., 14
  comparisons to, 4-6, 9, 10, 12 *n.*, 17, 23-25, 27, 29, 31 *n.*, 36, 39, 43-45 *n.*, 50 *n.*, 53, 54, 56-59, 61, 63, 64, 66, 74, 75, 77, 83-85, 87-89, 91, 92
  influences from, 3, 10, 31

United States (*Continued*)
  non-recognition, 39
  oil companies, 47
Universities, 82
Urabe Hyakutaro, 69 *n.*

Vakil, C. N., 15 *n.*
Veterans, relief for, 55
Vocational ability, compulsory registration of, 52
Vocational schools, 82

Wages, 51, 55
Wakatsuki Cabinet, 67, 73
Wakatsuki Reijiro, Premier, 27
Walker, Melville H., 26 *n.*
Wallace, U. S. Secretary of Agriculture, 29
Wang Au-shih, 29
War Cabinet (Great Britain), 69 *n.*
War Industries Board (U. S.), 50 *n.*
War Policies Commission (U. S.), 50 *n.*
Waseda University, 82
Watanabe, Inspector-General of Military Education, 78
Webb-Pomerene Export Trade Act (U. S.), 12 *n.*, 23
Weekly Bulletin (Japanese periodical), 83, 90, 91
Woman suffrage, 74
Wool and woolens, 15-17, 37, 38
World War, effects, 6-8, 10

Yabe Tadaharu, 73 *n.*
Yamagata Aritomo, elder statesman, 78
Yanase Ryokan, 44 *n.*, 77 *n.*
Yasuda, capitalist, 26
Yasuo Nagaharu, 22 *n.*, 42 *n.*
Yawata Iron Works, 45
Yonai Cabinet, 68, 73
Young Men's Associations, 83
Youth schools, 56
Yuki, Minister of Finance, 28

Zaigo Gunjin Kai: See Reservists' Association

LIST OF STATUTES CITED

Arukoru Sembai Ho, Alcohol Monopoly Law, 47
Beikoku Haikyu Tosei Ho, Rice Distribution Control Law, 30
Beikoku Ho, Rice Law, 29
Beikoku Jichi Kanri Ho, Rice Autonomous Control Law, 30
Beikoku no Okyu Sochi ni Kansuru Horitsu, Law in regard to Temporary Rice Measures, 30 *n.*
Beikoku Tosei Ho, Rice Control Law, 29-30, 32
Beikoku Tosei nado Seigen Rei, Rice Hulling, etc., Restriction Ordinance, 51
Boeki Chosetsu oyobi Tsusho Yogo ni Kansuru Horitsu, Trade Protection Law, 16
Boeki oyobi Kankei Sangyo no Chosei ni Kansuru Horitsu, Law Concerning Adjustment of Foreign Trade and Industries Related Thereto, 18
Chian Iji Ho, Peace Preservation Law, 72, 83, 84, 86
Chinkin Rinji Sochi Rei, Ordinance for Emergency Regulation of Wages, 51
Chinkin Tosei Rei, Wage Control Ordinance, 51
Dai Nippon Koku Kabushiki Kaisha Ho, Japan Aviation Company Law, 48
Denryoku Chosei Rei, Ordinance for Control of Electric Power, 51
Denryoku Kanri Ho, Electric Power Control Law, 49
Dogyo Kumiai Junsoku, Standard Rules for Joint Occupation Associations, 11
Fudosan Yushi oyobi Sonshitsu Hosho Ho, Law for Credits on Immovables and for Indemnification for Losses, 35
Fuon Bunsho Rinji Torishimari Ho, Seditious Literature Emergency Control Law, 86
Gaikasai Tokubetsu-zei Ho, Foreign Currency Bonds Special Tax Law, 60

Gaikoku Kawase Kanri Ho, Foreign Exchange Control Law, 17, 18
Gakko Ginosha Yosei Rei, School Technician Training Ordinance, 52
Gakko Sotsugyo-sha Shiyo Seigen Rei, University and School Graduates Employment Limitation Ordinance, 51
Gen San Shu Kanri Ho, Silk Worm Eggs Control Law, 32
Giin-ho, Law of the Houses, 76
Gunju Kogyo Doin Ho, Military Supplies Industries Mobilization Law, 44
Gunki Hogo Ho, Military Secrets Protection Law, 86
Gunma Shigen Hogo Ho, Military Horses Resources Protection Law, 53
Gunyo Jidosha Hojo Ho, Military Motor Vehicles Subsidy Law, 46
Gunyo Kobutsu Lo-an Ho, Law for Increase of Production of Minerals for Military Use, 53
Gunyo Shigen Himitsu Hogo Ho, Military Resources Secrets Protection Law, 86
Hiryo Kanri Ho An, Fertilizer Control Bill, 34
Hojin Shihon-zei Ho, Juridical Persons Capital Tax Law, 60
Hoku-Shi Jiken Tokubetsu-zei Ho, North China Affair Special Tax Law, 60
Hokuyo Gyogyo Torishimari Ho, North Seas Fishery Supervision Law, 22
Iryo Kankei-sha Noryoku Shinkoku Rei, Medical Professional Ability Registration Ordinance, 52
Jidai Yachin Tosei Rei, Ordinance for the Control of Ground and House Rents, 52
Jidosha Kotsu Jigyo Ho, Motor Vehicles Communications Industry Law, 46
Jinji Chotei Ho, Domestic Disputes Conciliation Law, 35 *n.*

111

LIST OF STATUTES CITED

Jinzo Sekiyu Seizo Jigyo Ho, Artificial Oil Manufacture Undertakings Law, 47

Juishi Shokugyo Noryoku Shinkoku Rei, Veterinary Profession Ability Registration Ordinance, 52

Juyo Bussan Dogyo Kumiai Ho, Staple Commodities Guilds Law, 11, 26

Juyo Hiryo Gyo Tosei Ho, Staple Fertilizers Industry Control Law, 34

Juyo Sangyo Tosei Ho, Major Industries Control Law, 25, 27, 28, 45, 46

Juyo Yushutsu Hin Dogyo Kumiai Ho, Staple Exports Guilds Law, 11, 26

Juyo Yushutsu Hin Kogyo Kumiai Ho, Staple Export Commodities Industrial Guilds Law, 26

Juyo Yushutsu Hin Kogyo Kumiai Ho, Staple Exports Industrial Guilds Law, 12

Kaigun Kyuyo Rei, Naval Supplies Ordinance, 44

Kaisha Rieki Haito oyobi Shikin Yutsu Rei, Company Profit, Dividend, and Capital Financing Ordinance, 51

Kaisha Shokuin Kyuyo Rinji Sochi Rei, Ordinance for Emergency Regulation of the Supply of Corporate Employees, 52

Kakaku nado Tosei Rei, Ordinance for the Control of Prices, etc., 52

Kani Seimei Hoken Ho, Post Office Life Insurance Law, 56 n.

Kei Kinzoku Seizo Jigyo Ho, Light Metals Manufacture Undertakings Law, 53

Kikaku-in Kansei, Planning Board Statute, 66 n.

Kinsen Saimu Rinji Chotei Ho, Monetary Debts Conciliation Law, 35

Kizoku-in-rei, House of Peers Ordinance, 75, 76

Koeki Shichiya Ho, Public Pawn Shops Law, 56 n.

Kogyo Ho, Mining Act, 55

Kogyo Kumiai Ho, Industrial Guilds Law, 26

Kojo Ho, Factory Act, 55

Kojo Jigyojo Ginosha Yosei Rei, Factory and Workshop Technician Training Ordinance, 52

Kojo Jigyojo Kanri Rei, Factory and Workshop Supervision Ordinance, 52

Kojo Shugyo Jikan Seigen Rei, Factory Working Hours Limitation Ordinance, 51

Kokka Sodoin Ho, General Mobilization Law, 32, 40, 50-53, 55-56, 62, 68, 69, 80

Kokka Sodoin Ho nado no Shikko no Tokatsu ni Kansuru Ken, Ordinance regarding Invocation of the General Mobilization Law, 69 n.

Kokka Sodoin Shingi-kai Rei, General Mobilization Commission Ordinance, 52

Kokuki Seizo Jigyo Ho, Airplane Manufacture Industries Law, 48

Kokumin Choyo Rei, National Conscription Ordinance, 51

Kokumin Kenko Hoken Ho, National Health Insurance Law, 56

Kokumin Shokugyo Noryoku Shinkoku Rei, National Vocational Ability Registration Ordinance, 52

Koro Tosei Ho, Navigation Routes Control Law, 21

Kosaku Chotei Ho, Farm Tenancy Conciliation Law, 35 n.

Kosaku Kikai Jigyo Ho, Machine Tools Undertakings Law, 52

Menorimono Indo Yushutsu Shomei Kisoku, Rules for Certification of Cotton Goods Exports to India, 15

Menseihin Tosei Ho, Cotton Goods Control Law, 43

Momi Kyodo Chozo Josei Ho, Law for Aid to Cooperative Storage of Unhulled Rice, 30

Nippon Hasso Den Kabushiki Kaisha Ho, Japan Electric Power Generation and Transmission Company Law, 49

Nippon Sanki Shinko Kabushiki Kaisha Ho, Japan Gold Production Encouragement Corporation Law, 59 n.

Nochi Chosei Ho, Farm Lands Adjustment Law, 36

Nogyo Dosan Shinyo Ho, Agricultural Chattel Credit Law, 35-36

Nogyo Hoken Ho, Agricultural Insurance Law, 36

LIST OF STATUTES CITED

Nogyo Saihoken Tokubetsu Kaikei Ho, Agricultural Re-insurance Special Accounts Law, 36

Noka Fusai Seiri Kumiai Ho, Farm Household Debt Adjustment Cooperatives Law, 35

Noson Fusai Seiri Ho, Farm Village Debt Adjustment Law, 35

Rinji Hiryo Haikyu Tosei Ho, Temporary Fertilizer Distribution Control Law, 34

Rinji Naikaku Sangi Kansei, Emergency Cabinet Councillors Statute, 68 n.

Rinji Noson Fusai Shori Ho, Temporary Farm Debts Settlement Law, 36

Rinji Sempaku Kanri Ho, Emergency Shipping Control Law, 21, 50

Rinji Shikin Chosei Ho, Emergency Capital Adjustment Law, 19, 50, 59

Rinji Sozei Zocho Ho, Temporary Tax Increase Law, 60

Rodo Sogi Chotei Ho, Labor Disputes Conciliation Law, 35 n., 55

Ryusan Ammonia Zosan oyobi Haikyu Tosei Ho, Law for Increase of Production and Control of Distribution of Ammonium Sulphate, 35

San Ken Shori Tosei Ho, Cocoon Disposal Control Law, 32

San Shi Gyo Ho, Silk Industry Law, 30

San Shi Gyo Kumiai Ho, Silk Industry Guilds Law, 31

Sei Shi Gyo Ho, Silk Reeling Industry Law, 32

Sekiyu Shigen Kaihatsu Ho, Petroleum Resources Development Law, 47-48

Sempaku Unko Ginosha Yosei Rei, Marine Navigation Technician Training Ordinance, 52

Sen-in Ho, Mariners Act, 55

Sen-in Saitei Nenrei Ho, Seamen's Minimum Age and Health Certificate Act, 55

Sen-in Shokugyo Noryoku Shinkoku Rei, Seamen's Vocational Ability Registration Ordinance, 52

Shakuchi Shakuya Chotei Ho, Rented Lands and Houses Conciliation Law, 35 n.

Shasai Tampo Ken Shintaku Ho, Corporate Debenture Mortgage Trusteeship Law, 42-43

Shigen Chosa Ho, Resources Investigation Law, 44-45

Shihon Tohi Boshi Ho, Capital Flight Prevention Law, 17

Shika Antei Shisetsu Ho, Silk Price Stabilization Arrangements Law, 32

Shika Antei Shisetsu Tokubetsu Kaikei Ho, Silk Price Stabilization Special Accounts Law, 32

Shika Antei Yushi Hosho Ho, Silk Price Stabilization Credits Guarantee Law, 31

Shika Antei Yushi Sonshitsu Zengo Shori Ho, Law for Remedial Disposition of Losses on Silk Price Stabilization Loans, 31

Shika Antei Yushi Tampo Sei Shi Baishu Ho, Law for Purchase of Silk Held as Security for Silk Price Stabilization Loans, 31

Shiryo Haikyu Tosei Ho, Resources Distribution Control Law, 53

Shogyo Kumiai Ho, Commercial Guilds Law, 27

Shoji Chotei Ho, Commercial Matters Conciliation Law, 35 n.

Shoko Kumiai Chuo Kinko Ho, Central Depository for Commercial and Industrial Guilds Law, 27 n.

Shokuin Kenko Hoken Ho, Office Workers Health Insurance Law, 57

Sodoin Gyomu Jigyo Setsubi Rei, General Mobilization Enterprises Installations Ordinance, 52

Sodoin Gyomu Jigyoshu Keikaku Rei, Ordinance Regarding Planning by Directors of General Mobilization Enterprises, 52

Sodoin Gyomu Shitei Rei, General Mobilization Enterprise Designation Ordinance, 51

Sodoin Hosho Iinkai, General Mobilization Indemnification Commission Regulations, 52

Sodoin Shiken Kenkyu Rei, General Mobilization Experiment and Research Ordinance, 52

Teikoku Kogyo Kaihatsu Kabushiki Kaisha Ho, Imperial Mining Development Company Law, 53

Teikoku Nenryo Kogyo Kabushiki Kaisha Ho, Imperial Fuel Industry Company Law, 47

LIST OF STATUTES CITED

Tekko Haikyu Tosei Kisoku, Iron and Steel Distribution Control Regulations, 45-46

Tekko Tosei Ho, Iron and Steel Control Law, 42

Yatoiire Seigen Rei, Employment Limitation Ordinance, 51

Yuka Shoken Iten-zei Ho, Negotiable Securities Transfer Tax Law, 60

Yushutsu Kumiai Ho, Export Guilds Law, 12, 13, 26

Yushutsu Sei Shi Kensa Ho, Export Silk Inspection Law, 30

Yushutsu Sei Shi Torihiki Ho, Export Silk Transactions Law, 32

Yushutsunyu Rinji Sochi Ho, Emergency Imports Exports Management Law, 19